# JOHN KEATS

## 1795–1995

WITH A

CATALOGUE

OF THE HARVARD

KEATS COLLECTION

The Houghton Library

1995

ISBN 914630-17-2

Published on the occasion of the exhibition
*John Keats and the Exaltation of Genius*
5 September–28 October 1995
and of the
John Keats Bicentennial Conference
7–9 September 1995
The Houghton Library

This catalogue was made possible by a grant from
The Carl and Lily Pforzheimer Foundation

FRONT COVER:
JOSEPH SEVERN. Portrait of John Keats.
Pen and ink on paper, [ca. 1830]
(Keats *65M-13)
Gift of Arthur A. Houghton, Jr.

BACK COVER:
JOHN KEATS. "This living hand, now warm and capable."
Autograph manuscript, draft
(MS Keats 2.29.2).
Gift of Amy Lowell
This manuscript is the sole source for this text.

IN GRATITUDE

*Arthur A. Houghton, Jr.*
*(1906–1990)*

*and*

*Amy Lowell*
*(1874–1925)*

BENJAMIN ROBERT HAYDON. Diary entry for January 1817, including a profile sketch
of John Keats (lower right) done as a study for Haydon's painting "Christ's Entry into
Jerusalem" (fMS Eng 1331, vol VIII). Gift of Willard Pope, PhD 1932, in memory of his wife,
Evelyn Ryan Pope.

# Contents

# Preface

THERE IS PROBABLY no English writer—certainly no other English poet—as closely identified with the Houghton Library and Harvard University as John Keats. Keats's books and manuscripts were collected early and energetically at Harvard, and the room dedicated to his career was the only one of its kind to adorn the Library when it first opened in 1942. For collectors, Keats's name is intimately associated with that of Arthur A. Houghton, Jr., whose gift to the University made the Houghton Library possible. Romanticists realize, moreover, that Keats's achievement as a poet has long been the focus of scholarly attention in Cambridge, ranging from the ambitious biographical work of Amy Lowell and Walter Jackson Bate to the critical studies written by Bate, David Perkins, Helen Vendler, and James Engell. The Harvard University Press has served as Keats's principal publisher in the second half of this century, including the critical and facsimile editions edited by Jack Stillinger. It is therefore with considerable pleasure that my colleagues in the Houghton Library and I host the bicentennial conference devoted to Keats and offer this catalogue as a guide not just to our bicentenary exhibition but to Harvard's entire holdings of Keats's manuscripts.

The bicentennial conference has been organized under the auspices and with the support of the Keats-Shelley Association of America. I wish to express my gratitude both to William T. Buice III, the Association's extraordinarily able President, and to Professors Jack Stillinger, Robert Ryan, and Ronald Sharp, who carefully planned the conference proceedings, for their leadership and cooperation. Dennis Marnon, the Library's Administrative Officer, has handled local arrangements with his customary precision and aplomb.

The Library has marked John Keats's 200th birthday by mounting three separate exhibitions. The principal exhibition, conceived by Lisa Ronthal, a Teaching Fellow in the Department of English and American Literature at Harvard, is entitled "Keats and the Exaltation of Genius." The essay in this volume by Helen Vendler, the A. Kingsley Porter University Professor, draws together and enlivens the objects selected by Lisa Ronthal; I am deeply grateful to both of them for their crucial contributions. The exhibition itself was brought to the cases by Leslie A. Morris, Curator of Manuscripts in the Harvard College Library. A new exhibition of manuscripts and related materials in the Keats Room has been curated by Walter Jackson Bate, the A. Kingsley Porter University Professor *Emeritus*, to whom we are also indebted for his labors in organizing the iconography collection devoted to Keats. A third exhibition, in the Widener Library Rotunda, displays the Irish artist Ross Wilson's drawing and print studies after Keats's life mask. I wish to thank Peter Accardo, Vicki Denby, Elizabeth Falsey, and Bonnie B. Salt for their assistance in helping to install these exhibitions and prepare this catalogue.

As I have said, this volume is unusual in that it combines two essays—W. H. Bond's on the history of the Keats collections at Harvard, Helen Vendler's on the sociability of Keats's poetical career--with a complete catalogue of our holdings of Keats's manuscripts. This catalogue was prepared in the early 1970s by Bill Bond, my distinguished predecessor as Librarian of the Houghton Library, and I am delighted that his painstaking work can now be shared with a larger audience. This is possible in large part because Leslie Morris has carefully revised it, bringing it up to date to correspond with recently published reference works. I want to express my warmest appreciation of Leslie Morris's central role in preparing this catalogue and in organizing our various exhibitions.

The publication of this volume has been made possible by a generous grant from the Carl and Lily Pforzheimer Foundation. It gives me great pleasure to thank the Foundation, Carl H. Pforzheimer, Jr., and Carl Pforzheimer III, for the continuing support they have provided both Harvard University and the Keats-Shelley Association during the past many years.

Richard Wendorf

LIBRARIAN

# John Keats, 1795–1821: John Keats, 1795–1995

Where's the Poet? Show him! show him!

— JOHN KEATS

THE CELEBRATION OF THE BICENTENNIAL of Keats's birth in 1795 is in reality a celebration of his extraordinary continuing presence. No vanished author seems younger and fresher on the page. The weight of textual studies, of annotation, of contextualization, accumulates unceasingly, but Keats's writing moves easily out of its scholarly slipcase and warms into new being under the scrutiny of each generation. Two hundred years after Keats's birth, we can apply to him his own words about Homer: "His soul looks out through renovated eyes" ["Ode to Apollo"].[1]

Each poem of Keats arises from art as well as from circumstance. It is the aim of this exhibition to suggest both of these matrices—the life-events that brought his poetry to birth, and the arts (whether painting and sculpture, music, or earlier poetry) from which his own creation took its measure. In the case of some artists, the life is so circumscribed that it can be briefly told. But Keats's genius for family love and for friendship meant that his life, however short, was filled with people, with incident, and with letters. A life of such human affection generated an art that was above all social and communal. As he composed an early acrostic on the name of his sister-in-law Georgiana, he included the lines:

> Imagine not that greatest mastery
> And kingdom over all the realms of verse
> Nears more to heaven in aught than when we nurse
> And surety give to love and brotherhood.
> ["Give me your patience"]

It was not an accident that Keats wrote "I think I shall be among the English Poets after my death" [letter of 14–31 October 1818], envisaging himself posthumously in the company of fellow-poets rather than aloof in solitary fame. Because of his social openness, he went more eagerly than most lyric poets to encounter the large and impersonal realms of learning, medicine, politics, and travel. He had ambitions to replicate, as a playwright, the whole social world on the stage, as Shakespeare had done.

Yet for all his family attachment and his irrepressible social appetite, he was invisibly always tethered elsewhere—to "those abstractions which are my only life," as he himself

---

[1] Excerpts from Keats's letters are from *The Letters of John Keats, 1814–1821*, edited by Hyder Edward Rollins (Cambridge, Massachusetts, 1958). Quotations from poems follow *The Poems of John Keats*, edited by Jack Stillinger (Cambridge, Massachusetts, 1978). Item numbers in the text refer to the checklist of the exhibition.

wrote on 22 September 1818, as he attempted to escape from the "new strange and threaten-
ing sorrow" of his brother Tom's impending death. Those abstractions were in the first
instance the immemorial recourses of thought—suffering, the seasons, the female, historical
spectacle—and in the second instance the generic forms of poetry—the ode, the sonnet, the
quest-narrative. Thought and poetic form cross constantly in Keats. He knows that if the
philosophic mind is to be his, it has to be acquired through poetry, not outside of it. His only
guides in this perplexing quest are his predecessors in art—not only Shakespeare but the
Greek sculptors, not only Burns but Homer, not only Wordsworth but Raphael and Haydon.
He is a venerator, and on the Isle of Wight he puts up, above his books, a picture of
Shakespeare, his "Presider" [letter of 10, 11 May 1817]. Almost too much a venerator, he is
nearly unmanned by the Elgin marbles—"My spirit is too weak." Nonetheless, he summons
up courage even when he confronts the heroic scale of the Greeks; and it is a measure of his
own intimacy with aesthetic power that he eventually sees a grand leisure in intellectual
supremacy, representing it as "might half slumb'ring on its own right arm" ["Sleep and
Poetry"].

It is perhaps right that the first case in this exhibition shows us Keats in relation both to
art and to his contemporaries, the two so intertwined that they cannot be disentangled. He
thinks about Apollo, and a friend sends him a laurel wreath which he dares to place on his
own head; he is immediately scandalized (according to "God of the golden bow") at his own
complicity in this sacrilege ("like a blank ideot I put on thy wreath— / Thy laurel, thy
glory"), and yet he yearns (as he says in the sonnet "On Receiving a Laurel Crown from
Leigh Hunt") for the crowning to be authentic: "'tis nearly pain / To be conscious of such a
coronet." Around him, London has taken up fashionable Hellenism, but Keats has absorbed
it not as fashion but as revelation. Apollo takes on a palpable reality to him; as if by
metempsychosis, he becomes an avatar of Apollo—who is, significantly for a poet trained as
a physician, the god of medicine as well as of poetry. The urge to address Apollo becomes
irresistible, and "God of the golden bow" is written in part to calm it. Hellenism filled a void
that Keats had scarcely acknowledged—the evacuation of his early Christianity. His beauti-
fully simple letter of 31 March 1819 to his young sister Fanny—retailing the essence of the
catechism and quoting the prophets so that she could more easily learn her confirmation
lessons—shows how much Keats had retained of what he had been taught of Christian
belief. Yet his intemperate scorn of Christian practice (evident in his Shelleyan sonnet against
the "black spell" of "vulgar superstition") apparently drove out any remnants of adherence to
Christianity. Both his scientific training and his political radicalism removed him from
sympathy with established Christian institutions; his ardent idealism transferred itself to an
imagined Greek world of harmonious forms. When that world opened itself to him through
Chapman's translation of Homer, he burst out, "Then felt I like some watcher of the skies...."
The exhilaration is palpably felt, and suggests a perhaps unadmitted sense of deprivation
preceding it.

The sonnet on Homer—immensely precocious, intensely realized—depends on Keats's perception that there was a difference not in degree but in kind between the literature he knew and the *Odyssey* (from which he derived the sonnet's metaphors). Other poets were realms, states, islands; Homer was a rumored "expanse." Chapman speaks Homer from the page, and his transfigured reader feels like—like what? Like a watcher of the skies, discovering through his telescope a new planet named "Homer." Yet Keats rapidly passes over this simile as unsatisfactory, and replaces it by another: the reader is now "like stout Cortez," who discovers the Pacific. Why is discovering Homer more like coming upon a new ocean than like seeing a new planet? Because the astronomer cannot visit and explore his distant planet, whereas Cortez and his men can sail in and chart the Pacific. Also, the astronomer is alone, but Cortez is—as Keats almost always imagined himself being—one of a company. "Oft of one wide expanse *had I been told*": the readers of Homer make up a society constantly recruiting others, with Chapman (and through him, Keats) members of the group.

Just as a company of poets surrounds Keats in his imagination, so he imagines a company of readers making up the chorus of astonishment at Homer, looking at each other with a "wild surmise" on discovering the Homeric epics. These companies stand in opposition to the deluded sects joining in vulgar superstition. Keats's pugnacity in defending his own youthful values against a social superstructure he mistrusts (superstition, "the sermon's horrid sound," the feudal order, the state) will break into voice now and again throughout his writing life. But intemperateness was not a quality he approved of in himself; his poetry struggles to transform the contentiousness of anger into the more profound insight of tragedy, enacted most somberly in "The Fall of Hyperion."

It is Keats's vivacity, and even his pugnacity, that appear in his vivid face as sketched by his friend, the artist Benjamin Robert Haydon, in his painting "Christ's Entry into Jerusalem." No other representation of Keats so catches the spirited eagerness remarked on by all his friends. And Haydon's breadth of mind could inspire Keats in a way that the more limited talent of a Leigh Hunt could not. Haydon thought sublimely, and created grandly; and Keats's imperfect but undeluded sense of his own imaginative potential responded to Haydon's Shakespearean scale. It was chiefly through Haydon that Keats was brought to his own awe before the Elgin marbles. The recently-acquired marbles were of course the subject of wide discussion; and Keats would publish the "Ode on a Grecian Urn" in the *Annals of the Fine Arts*, where the marbles were commended in reverential terms. But very few of those visiting the special exhibition rooms where the marbles were displayed were as competent as Haydon (who had campaigned vigorously for the purchase of the works by the nation) to discern their technical greatness as sculpture. And few listening to Haydon's responses—as he praised in Phidias "the combination of Nature with idea"—would have been so receptive as Keats, who was to conceive of the marbles as mingling "with a billowy main— / A sun—a shadow of a magnitude." Haydon's letter after receiving Keats's sonnets on the Elgin marbles— "Many thanks my dear fellow for your two noble sonnets—. . . You filled me with fury for an hour, and with admiration for ever"—stands in this exhibition as one of the first adequate recognitions of Keats's imaginative strength.

In spite of the pediment sculptures of the Parthenon having been intended as represen-
tations of the gods, they are so bare of divine attributes, in their ruined state, that they
appear human rather than divine; and yet their majestic proportions suggest an ambitious
humanism of more than human dimensions, just as the measured grace of the Panathenaic
procession hints at a voluntary (even aesthetic) obedience to Fate that displaces tragedy in
favor of an exalted understanding. Finally, the many metopes narrating the combat between
Lapiths and Centaurs represent, in a mode exciting to Keats, how the submerged violence of
erotic desire could rise to a life-and-death struggle in the pursuit of sexual conquest.

The Elgin marbles stood as a perpetual end-point in Keats's imagination. Many of the
figures in the "Ode on a Grecian Urn" seem to arise literally from scenes on the Parthenon:

> Who are these coming to the sacrifice?
>     To what green altar, O mysterious priest,
>     Lead'st thou that heifer lowing at the skies. . . ?

But in their last manifestation in Keats's work, the marbles, disposed in recumbent grace, are
wholly naturalized:

> Sometimes whoever seeks abroad may find
> Thee sitting careless on a granary floor,
>     Thy hair soft-lifted by the winnowing wind;
> Or on a half-reap'd furrow sound asleep,
>     Drows'd with the fume of poppies, . . .
>                 ["To Autumn"]

The plastic imagination which could visualize such a tableau had not of course been
formed solely by sculpture. It had been nurtured in Keats's omnivorous and wholehearted
reading in both Spenser (his copy of Spenser is on exhibit [no.12]) and Milton. One expressive
means that Keats took from Spenser is the value of the "golden-tongued" tautological—of
an excess of statement over what is needed for purely informational purposes. Spenser never
says anything once; and any young poet, pondering the function of Spenserian repetition, is
soon led into the recesses and wildernesses of language, its elaborations and artifices. Keats
made luxurious adaptations of Spenserian effects in *Endymion*, "The Eve of St. Agnes" and
"Lamia," borrowing—in addition to archaic and profuse language and (in the "Eve")
prosody— Spenser's quest-motif, romance plot, and processional tableaux. When he forsook
Spenserian romance in favor of Shakespearean tragedy, it was with a felt pang:

> O golden-tongued Romance, with serene lute!
>     Fair plumèd syren, queen of far-away!
>     Leave melodizing on this wintry day,
> Shut up thine olden pages, and be mute.
> Adieu!
>         ["On Sitting Down to Read *King Lear* Once Again"]

This is the first of Keats's stern adieus, which figure so strongly, thematically and verbally, in the odes:

> Adieu! the fancy cannot cheat so well
>    As she is fam'd to do, deceiving elf.
> Adieu! adieu! thy plaintive anthem fades . . .
>          ["Ode to a Nightingale"]

If (for Keats) Spenser was Fancy, and Shakespeare was Imagination, then Milton was Politics. It is notable that all three of these precursors were poets of society; none was a purely lyric writer. And Keats's ambition was directed toward the social imagination, which he at first believed to be one inflected by politics. Keats was eventually to repudiate Milton's Latinity of style ("Life to him would be death to me," as he said in his mammoth journal-letter of 17–27 September 1819), but he never ceased to admire Milton's intellect (remarked on in the exhibited letter to James Rice [no. 13]) as well as his architectonic "stationing" of figures in space. That "stationing" is political as well as geometrical: Milton's hierarchies of territory and of authority shape the political world of his epic. We can see Keats imitating such dynastic and hierarchical "stationing" in "Hyperion"—his re-staging of *Paradise Lost*—with figures from the Elgin marbles, showing the aged and infirm Titans overthrown by the superior Olympians. As the Titan Oceanus perceives, "on our heels a fresh perfection treads": Keats's epic echoes the improved world of *Paradise Lost*, but secularizes and Hellen–izes it.

Keats's uneven but convincing poem "Lines on Seeing a Lock of Milton's Hair" (in-cluded in the exhibited letter to Bailey [no. 14]) conveys, through its symbol, the combina-tion of startled awareness and prophetic pre-cognition felt by an author encountering a peculiarly cognate fellow writer. Keats is unnerved when he is shown, by the poet and editor Leigh Hunt, this actual material remnant of Milton. Pressed by Hunt to write about it, Keats expresses his surprise at seeing the lock, but at the same time feels he has known Milton since the foundations of time:

> A lock of thy bright hair—
>    Sudden it came,
> And I was startled, when I caught thy name
>    Coupled so unaware;
> Yet at the moment, temperate was my blood—
> Methought I had beheld it from the Flood.

The awkwardness of Keats's poem is the formal correlative to the embarrassment one feels before a literary relic; it is, and it is not, from the same world as the literary object. The Houghton Library's enshrined lock of Keats's hair has something of the aura of hair rings and hair brooches, of attics and Victoriana; yet its auburn reality can still cause an emotion resembling the one Keats felt, taken aback, before the lock of Milton's hair.

Keats's veneration for Shakespeare had none of the ambivalence of his admiration for Milton. His love of Shakespeare never waned, and his insight into both the poems and the plays is unmatched. He read and reread Shakespeare; he marked Shakespeare; he imitated Shakespeare; he "burned through" Shakespearean tragedy; he defended (by marginalia in his volumes of Johnson's Shakespeare [no. 25]) Shakespeare against Johnson's criticisms; he absorbed (through Hazlitt especially) a lively sense of Shakespearean characterization. Had Keats lived, Shakespeare's plays would have continued more and more to saturate his poetry. As it is, Shakespeare's narrative poems and sonnets had the most visible effect on Keats's lyrics. Though Keats rebelled against the sonnet form as Shakespeare had used it (disliking the "pouncing" effect of the final couplet), he was deeply interested in Shakespeare's meta-phorical fertility: the sonnets, he said, were "full of fine things said unintentionally— in the intensity of working out conceits" [letter to J. H. Reynolds of 22 November 1817]. He also pondered the component units of sonnets—quatrains, sestets, octaves—and experimented with recombining them. In the chief odes, he based his stanzas on a Shakespearean quatrain combined with a Petrarchan sestet—a form lengthened by an extra, penultimate line in the lingering valedictions of "To Autumn" [no. 11]:

> Season of mists and mellow fruitfulness,
>   Close bosom-friend of the maturing sun;
> Conspiring with him how to load and bless
>   With fruit the vines that round the thatch-eaves run;
> To bend with apples the moss'd cottage-trees,
>   And fill all fruit with ripeness to the core;
>     To swell the gourd, and plump the hazel shells
>   With a sweet kernel; to set budding more,
> And still more, later flowers for the bees,
> Until they think warm days will never cease,
>     For summer has o'er-brimm'd their clammy cells.

But before these opulent redeployments of sonnet-units, Keats had been drawn to Shakespeare's "Venus and Adonis" as an example of a poem narrating not the heroic deeds of epic, but rather the trials of erotic passion. Shakespeare's brisk comedy in "Venus and Adonis" was still beyond Keats; it was with a high idealism that Keats retold his much-elaborated version of the tale of the Greek shepherd Endymion's love for the moon-goddess Cynthia. Keats's youthful Endymion, as he searches for his vanished Cynthia, makes a cosmological journey under the earth, under the sea, and through the skies, troubled by his inability to choose between his human love (the Indian maid Peona) and the celestial Cynthia. In under-taking *Endymion*, Keats had determined to exert his own powers by composing a long poem:

—it will be a test, a trial of my Powers of Imagination. . . . I must make
4000 Lines of one bare circumstance and fill them with Poetry; . . . [A] long
Poem is a test of Invention which I take to be the Polar Star of Poetry, as
Fancy is the Sails, and Imagination the Rudder.

[letter of 8 October 1817 [no. 23]]

When, in his next letter, Keats apportions "a little Pæòna Wife" to his friend Benjamin
Bailey, we can only conclude that his own taste favors Cynthia; yet he included the Indian
maid in his idyll because he suspected he would come in time to a higher valuing of terres-
trial things. He confessed in a letter that he had been moulting his "wings" in favor of a pair
of "patient sublunary legs." By his final merging of Cynthia and Peona into one person, he
evaded, in *Endymion,* the issue of choice between the superlunary and the sublunary. It was
not until he wrote his autumn ode that he discovered how to make that choice superfluous,
as he came to see the human as the origin of the divine.

When Keats descended from the mythological to the earthly, it was to use those patient
sublunary legs for a long walking tour of Scotland in the summer of 1818, during which he
(with his friend Charles Armitage Brown) visited Robert Burns's birthplace. Keats's imagina-
tion was moved by Burns's humble origins, his spontaneity of song, his suffering, and his
premature death. The long letters Keats wrote from Scotland to his brother Tom, his sister
Fanny, and his friends leave a memorable record of the genesis of several poems. As he
jocularly summed up the journey to the mother of his sister-in-law Georgiana,

I have been *werry* romantic indeed, among these Mountains & Lakes. I
have got wet through day after day, eaten oat cake, & drank whiskey,
walked up to my knees in Bog, got a sore throat, . . . went up Ben Nevis, &
N.B. came down again; . . . Besides riding about 400, we have walked above
600 Miles.

[letter of 6 August 1818]

He saw Ailsa Rock, and Staffa, and Mull, and climbed Ben Nevis, the highest peak in Britain
("it is almost like a fly crawling up a wainscoat," he told his brother Tom on 3 August). The
climb evoked the saddest poem of the journey from the "thin and fevered" Keats (Charles
Brown's words in a 7 August letter to Charles Wentworth Dilke). It is Keats's great
Shakespearean sonnet of scepticism, taking as its metaphor the mists that stretched in all
directions at the top of Ben Nevis, impeding any view. I give it as it appears in the letter
of 3–6 August to Tom:

After a little time the Mist cleared away but still there were large Clouds about attracted by old Ben to a certain distance so as to form as it were and large dome curtains which kept sailing about, opening and shutting at intervals here and there and everywhere; so that although we did not see one vast wide extent of prospect all round we saw something perhaps finer — these cloud veils opening with a dissolving motion and showing us the mountainous region beneath as through a loop hole — these mostly loop holes ever varying and discovering fresh prospect east west north and south — Then it was misty again and again it was fair — then puff came a cold breeze of wind and blew me a craggy shape [...]

JOHN KEATS. Autograph letter signed to Tom Keats, 3 August 1818, including a draft of "Read me a lesson, Muse, and speak it loud" (MS Keats 1.36). Gift of Arthur A. Houghton, Jr.

> Read me a Lesson muse, and speak it loud
> Upon the top of Nevis blind in Mist!
> I look into the Chasms and a Shroud
> Vaprous doth hide them; just so much I wist
> Mankind do know of Hell: I look o'erhead
>    And there is sullen Mist; even so much
> Mankind can tell of Heaven: Mist is spread
>    Before the Earth beneath me—even such
> Even so vague is Man's sight of himself.
>    Here are the craggy Stones beneath my feet;
> Thus much I know, that a poor witless elf
>    I tread on them; that all my eye doth meet
>      Is mist and Crag—not only on this height
>      But in the World of thought and mental might—

Mist remained the moral import of the Scottish journey; but Keats was also scrawling a brisk travelogue as he went along, finding even the reverential visit to Burns's birthplace a locus of irritable comedy:

> We went to the Cottage and took some Whiskey—I wrote a sonnet for the mere sake of writing some lines under the roof—they are so bad I cannot transcribe them—The Man at the Cottage was a great Bore with his Anecdotes—I hate the rascal—. . . he is a mahogany faced old Jackass who knew Burns—He ought to be kicked for having spoken to him . . .—O the flummery of a birth place! Cant! Cant! Cant! It is enough to give a spirit the guts-ache— . . . The flat dog made me write a flat sonnet—
>                        [letter to Reynolds of 11–13 July 1818]

Keats's judgment on his poem written at Burns's cottage was accurate; but he had earlier composed (as he wrote to Tom) "in a strange mood, half asleep" a better sonnet, "On Visiting the Tomb of Burns." His mind was on Tom; and the sonnet, enclosed in a letter to Tom of 29 June–2 July, is almost a message to his dying brother:

> The shortlived, paly summer is but won
> From winters ague, for one hours gleam;
> Through saphire warm, their stars do never beam,
> All is cold Beauty; pain is never done.

Keats's rage at human misery reached its apogee as he and Brown walked across northern Ireland: "A Scotch cottage, though in that some times the Smoke has no exit but at the door, is a pallace to an irish one." Even in the worst scenes of Irish degradation, his intuitive sympathy found matter that interested him, as in his rapid sketch of a "Duchess of Dunghill" carried in her "sedan" chair:

It is no laughing matter tho—Imagine the worst dog kennel you ever saw
placed upon two poles from a mouldy fencing—In such a wretched thing
sat a squalid old Woman squat like an ape half starved from a scarcity of
Buiscuit in its passage from Madagascar to the cape,—with a pipe in her
mouth and looking out with a round-eyed skinny lidded, inanity—with a
sort of horizontal idiotic movement of her head—squab and lean she sat
and puff'd out the smoke while two ragged tattered Girls carried her
along—What a thing would be a history of her Life and sensations.

[letter to Tom Keats of 3–9 July 1818]

Imaginative, fluent, and unembarrassed notes of this sort testify to what a striking writer
Kcats always was, in prose as well as in verse.

If Burns was Keats's chosen eighteenth-century poet, Wordsworth was the living
precursor Keats most admired:

Great spirits now on earth are sojourning;
  He of the cloud, the cataract, the lake,
  Who on Helvellyn's summit, wide awake,
Catches his freshness from archangel's wing:

So Keats had written in his letter of 21 November 1816 to Haydon [no. 28]. He sent
Wordsworth a copy of his 1817 *Poems* inscribed "To W. Wordsworth with the Author's sincere
Reverence." In 1817, as his November letter to Benjamin Bailey shows, he was
working out the Wordsworthian theory of the creative Imagination in his own terms. Later,
on the 1818 walking trip, he called on Wordsworth (to whom he had been introduced by
Haydon in 1817), only to find—as he told George and Georgiana in the June letter exhibited
here [no. 29]—that the poet was not at home. Keats admired Wordsworth most deeply for
having been able to penetrate into the darker chambers of consciousness, beyond the
"infant or thoughtless Chamber," beyond the "Chamber of Maiden-Thought," to the "dark
passages" where "We see not the ballance of good and evil. We are in a Mist":

To this point was Wordsworth come, as far as I can conceive when he
wrote 'Tintern Abbey' and it seems to me that his Genius is explorative of
those dark Passages. . . . Here I must think Wordsworth is deeper than
Milton.

[letter to Reynolds of 3 May 1818]

Keats's immense receptivity to suffering eventuated in his praise of Negative Capabil-
ity— "when a man is capable of being in uncertainties, Mysteries, doubts, without any
irritable reaching after fact & reason" [letter to George and Tom Keats of 21, 27[?] December
1817]. It was perhaps inevitable that as Keats's own confidence grew, he would find out his
differences from Wordsworth, expressed in the famous letter of 27 October 1818 [no. 30],
where he defines the poetical character, and distinguishes it from the Wordsworthian "ego-
tistical sublime":

As to the poetical Character itself, (I mean that sort of which, if I am any thing, I am a Member; that sort distinguished from the wordsworthian or egotistical sublime; which is a thing per se and stands alone) it is not itself—it has no self—it is every thing and nothing—It has no character—it enjoys light and shade; it lives in gusto, be it foul or fair, high or low, rich or poor, mean or elevated—It has as much delight in conceiving an Iago as an Imogen. What shocks the virtuous philosop[h]er, delights the camelion Poet.

This defiantly aesthetic passage—designed to shock the virtuous Wordsworth as much as the virtuous philosopher—goes on to defend its fundamentally Shakespearean conception of poetry as a form of thought-experiment, something which ends "in speculation" rather than in moral propositions. Keats's inclination towards empathy with many forms of being (derived from Shakespeare via Hazlitt) contrasts dramatically with Wordsworth's emphasis on the development of his own mind as a type of the growth of human consciousness. The genre serving as background to Keats is the drama, in which the author is invisible; the genre serving as background to Wordsworth is the Protestant conversion-autobiography, in which the salvation of a single soul is at stake. Keats was of course unfair to Wordsworth, but he was acting in the service of his own aesthetic conviction, indispensable to his own self-actualizing as an artist.

Attracted as he was to Shakespeare, Spenser, and Wordsworth, Keats still looked beyond the English poets to the first great poet of the European vernacular, Dante. He carried his three little volumes of Cary's translation of the *Comedy* with him on the Scottish trip, and "The Fall of Hyperion" would never have assumed its severity of purgatorial inquiry without the example of Dante. The transmutation of Dante's quest (crossed with Milton's Genesis) in the Induction of "The Fall of Hyperion" gives the poem a sublimity of tone unlike anything else in Keats.

A lesser, erotic, version of Dante's influence can be seen in Keats's dream-sonnet, where his spirit, flying to "that second circle of sad Hell," becomes Paolo, swirling with Francesca in the infernal wind:

> Pale were the sweet lips I saw,
> Pale were the lips I kiss'd, and fair the form
> I floated with, about that melancholy storm.
> ["As Hermes once"]

Paolo and Francesca are one of the many embracing couples appearing throughout Keats's poetry: Endymion and Cynthia; the knight and the Belle Dame; Madeline and Porphyro. The only "perfect" couple is Love and Psyche (borrowed from both Spenser and Shakespeare, but owed in the first instance to Apuleius). As the "Ode to Psyche" [no. 34] enviously notes, Cupid and Psyche can clasp each other doubly: "Their arms embracèd, and their pinions too." And they can kiss and not kiss in an untiring love:

JOHN KEATS. Autograph letter signed to George and Georgiana Keats, 14–31 October 1818, including " 'Tis 'the witching time of night' " (MS Keats 1.39). Gift of Arthur A. Houghton, Jr.

They lay calm-breathing on the bedded grass;
   Their arms embracèd, and their pinions too;
   Their lips touch'd not, but had not bade adieu,
As if disjoinèd by soft-handed slumber,
And ready still past kisses to outnumber
   At tender eye-dawn of aurorean love:
     The wingèd boy I knew;
But who wast thou, O happy, happy dove?
     His Psyche true!

This first-completed of the great odes, an irregular poem that is Miltonic and Spenserian at once, ushered in the miraculous months of 1819 during which Keats composed "Ode on Indolence," "Ode to a Nightingale," "Ode on a Grecian Urn," "Ode on Melancholy," and "To Autumn."

In his lighter moments in 1818 and 1819, Keats tossed off several poems in tetrameter couplets, among them "Bards of passion and of mirth" [no. 32]. George and Georgiana Keats, in Kentucky, would open one of Keats's long journal-letters and find poems such as this one spilling over the densely-written page of lightweight paper. When Keats learned in 1818 that they were expecting a baby, he wrote, in a letter of 14–31 October [no. 37]:

> If I had a prayer to make for any great good, next to Tom's recovery, it should be that one of your Children should be the first American Poet. I have a great mind to make a prophecy and they say prophecies work out their own fulfillment.

The prophecy follows, and it includes the visionary lines:

Child! I see thee! Child I've found thee
Midst of the quiet all around thee! . . .
Child I know thee! Child no more
But a Poet *ever*more . . .
Little Child
O' the western wild
Bard art thou completely!—

Just as he is about to lose his younger brother to tuberculosis, Keats welcomes a new family member born in America. The prophecy is also a gesture of cultural colonizing, claiming the New World for poetry so that it will be a more hospitable place for English exiles.

Tom's end foreshadowed Keats's own. Neither the hospitality offered in England by Fanny Brawne's mother (who took Keats into her own house despite the social convention that would keep an engaged couple separate), nor the hospitality offered in Italy by the letter from Shelley here exhibited [no. 38], could avert Keats's despairing last weeks in Rome and his agonizing death. As Keats posthumously "became his admirers" (Auden's words on

Yeats), his poems became precious to younger writers—Dickens, Tennyson, Arnold, Swinburne, Morris, Emerson, Eliot, Amy Lowell. Their copies of Keats's poems have come to rest in the Houghton Library Keats collection, of which the nucleus was Amy Lowell's great assemblage of Keatsiana, gathered as she prepared to write her biography of Keats.

Since Amy Lowell's death, the Keats materials have grown into an archive housed in its own room, where the "Presider"—to adopt Keats's phrase about his portrait of Shakespeare—is a bronzed copy of the plaster life-mask of Keats made by Haydon in December 1816, when Keats was twenty-one. The Houghton archive is not static; T.S. Eliot's Keats—presented as a gift to his brother Henry Ware Eliot—will not be the last copy of the poetry to be deposited here as testimony to a later writer's admiration for Keats's work. There is no dearth of recent poets drawing from Keats: Elizabeth Bishop, James Merrill, Amy Clampitt, and Seamus Heaney come immediately to mind. Because the canon of literature is formed, slowly but surely, by the admiration felt by subsequent writers for earlier ones, the closing case in this exhibition, in its display of the many copies of Keats's poetry treasured by his successors, testifies perhaps more eloquently than any other to the continued literary existence of a writer whose life on earth—1795 to 1821—was cruelly brief.

Helen Vendler

A. KINGSLEY PORTER UNIVERSITY PROFESSOR,
HARVARD UNIVERSITY

# John Keats and the Exaltation of Genius

## A checklist of the exhibition

*Unless otherwise noted, all items are by John Keats; in this list, manuscripts and letters are identified by their numbers in the Harvard Keats Collection catalogue, which provides source and provenance information.*

### I. EARLY EXALTATIONS

1. "Written in Disgust of Vulgar Superstition."
   Autograph manuscript of the first draft.
   MS Keats 2.10

2. *Poems*. London: Printed for C. & J. Ollier, 1817.
   Inscribed: "To J. H. Reynold's from his Friend J. Keats." With four sonnets in Keats's hand on pages [78] and [122].
   Gift of Arthur A. Houghton, Jr., 1950.
   Keats *EC8.K2262.817p (G)

3. "God of the golden bow."
   Autograph manuscript, draft with revisions.
   MS Keats 2.13

4. *The Western Messenger. Devoted to Religion and Literature*. Louisville: Western Unitarian Association; Boston: James Munroe & Co., 1835–1836. Volume 1.
   First printing of "God of the golden bow" from the manuscript presented to the editor by the poet's brother, 1 June 1836.
   Andover-Harvard Theological Library, SCR Period 2090

5. "On First Looking into Chapman's Homer."
   Autograph manuscript, early draft, differing from published version.
   MS Keats 2.4

6. *Poems*. London: Printed for C. & J. Ollier, 1817.
   Inscribed: "From J. K. to his affectionate Brother George." With two sonnets in George Keats's hand on the half-title page.
   Bequest of Amy Lowell, 1925.
   Keats *EC8.K2262.817p (D)

### II. HAYDON

7. Autograph letter, signed, to Benjamin Robert Haydon; [London] 20 November [1816].
   Contains an early version of the sonnet, "Addressed to the Same" (*Great spirits now on earth are sojourning*).
   MS Keats 1.3

8. Benjamin Robert Haydon.
   Autograph letter to John Keats; [London] 3 March 1817.
   MS Keats 4.7.2

9. Benjamin Robert Haydon.
   Diary: entry for 17 March 1817.
   Gift of Willard Bissell Pope in memory of his wife, Evelyn Ryan Pope, 1977.
   fMS Eng 1331 (10), Volume VIII, f. 73

10. Benjamin Robert Haydon. *Christ's Triumphant Entry into Jerusalem, by B. R. Haydon, Esq., Exhibited in London and Edinburgh, in the Year 1820. Exhibiting at the saloon of the Adelphi, South fifth street* . . . . Philadelphia: Printed by Charles Alexander, 1832.
    Acquired with funds presented by Willard

Bissell Pope in memory of his wife, Evelyn Ryan Pope, 1981.
*EC8.K2262.YHb846e

11. "To Autumn."
Autograph manuscript, early draft.
MS Keats 2.27

### III. Spenser & Milton

12. Edmund Spenser. *The Works of Mr. Edmund Spenser. In six volumes. With a glossary explaining the old and obscure words.* London: Printed for Jacob Tonson, 1715.
Keats's copy, with his markings and annotations.
Bequest of Amy Lowell, 1925.
Keats *EC8.K2262.Zz715s

13. Autograph letter to James Rice; Teignmouth [24 March 1818].
MS Keats 1.25

14. Autograph letter to Benjamin Bailey; [London] 23 January [1818].
MS Keats 1.20

15. Autograph letter to Jane and Mariane Reynolds; Oxford [4 September 1817]. Sealed with a cameo portrait of John Milton in black wax.
MS Keats 1.10

16. A lock of Keats's hair.
Gift of Arthur A. Houghton, Jr.

### IV. Shakespeare: Presiding Genius

17. Benjamin Robert Haydon.
Autograph letter to John Keats; [London] 4 March 1818.
MS Keats 4.7.8

18. Autograph letter to Benjamin Robert Haydon; Margate [10–11 May 1817], with annotation in Haydon's hand.
MS Keats 1.7

19. William Hazlitt. *Characters of Shakespear's Plays.* London: Printed by C. H. Reynell, for R. Hunter and C. and J. Ollier, 1817.
Keats's copy, with his autograph and annotations.
Bequest of Amy Lowell, 1925.
Keats *EC8.K2262.Zz817h

20. Zachariah Jackson. *Shakspeare's Genius Justified: Being restorations and illustrations of seven hundred passages in Shakspeare's plays: which have afforded abundant scope for critical animadversion; and hitherto held at defiance the penetration of all Shakspeare's commentators.* London: Printed by J. Johnson for John Major, 1819.
Keats's copy, with his annotations and inscription, "Wm. Haslam to John Keats."
Bequest of Amy Lowell, 1925.
Keats *EC8.K2262.Zz819j

21. Autograph letter to Benjamin Robert Haydon; Oxford, 28 September [1817]. Sealed with a cameo portrait of William Shakespeare in red wax.
MS Keats 1.12

### V. Shakespeare and *Endymion*

22. *Endymion: A Poetic Romance.* London: Printed for Taylor and Hessey, 1818.
Gift of Arthur A. Houghton, Jr., 1946.
Keats *EC8.K2262.818e (C)

23. Autograph letter to Benjamin Bailey; Hampstead [8] October [1817].
MS Keats 1.13

24. Autograph letter to Benjamin Bailey; [London, 28–30 October 1817].
Contains a version of *Endymion.*
MS Keats 1.14

25. William Shakespeare. *The Dramatic Works of William Shakspeare. . .Whittingham's edition.* Chiswick: Printed by C. Whittingham, 1814. 7 volumes.
Gift of Arthur A. Houghton, Jr., 1944.
Keats *EC8.K2262.Za814s

## VI. BURNS AND SCOTLAND

26. "There is a joy in footing slow across a silent plain." Autograph manuscript, draft.
MS Keats 2.19

27. *The Examiner, a Sunday paper, on politics, domestic economy, and theatricals, for the year 1822.* London: J. Hunt, 1822.
Includes "Lines Written in the Scotch Highlands."
Anonymous gift, 1941.
Keats *EC8.K2262.LEx15

## VII. WORDSWORTH AND ROMANTICISM

28. Autograph letter to Benjamin Robert Haydon; [London, 21 November 1816].
Contains revised version of "Addressed to the Same" (*Great spirits now on earth are sojourning*).
MS Keats 1.4

29. Autograph letter to George [and Georgiana] Keats; "foot of Helvellyn" 27[–28] June 1818.
Includes an account of a visit to Wordsworth's house.
MS Keats 1.32

30. Autograph letter to Richard Woodhouse; [Hampstead, 27 October 1818].
MS Keats 1.38

31. Autograph letter to Benjamin Bailey; [Dorking, 22 November 1817].
MS Keats 1.16

## VIII. FAMILY AND FRIENDS

32. Autograph letter to George and Georgiana Keats; [Hampstead, 16 December 1818–4 January 1819].
Includes "Bards of passion and of mirth."
MS Keats 1.45

33. Carlo Lasinio. *Pitture a fresco del Campo santo di Pisa. . . .* Firenze: Presso Molini, Landi e Campagno, 1812
Deposited by Mrs. James M. Hunnewell, 1963.
*63-417 PF

34. Autograph letter to George and Georgiana Keats;
[Hampstead] 14 February–3 May [1819].
Includes "Ode to Psyche" and "As Hermes once."
MS Keats 1.53

35. *The Indicator.* London: Printed for Joseph Appleyard, 1820. Volume I, No. XXXIX, p.304: "A dream after reading Dante's episode of Paulo and Francesca."
Gift of Arthur E. Davis, 1940.
Keats *EC8.H9135.LIn25

36. *Lamia, Isabella, The Eve of St. Agnes, and Other Poems.* London: Printed for Taylor and Hessey, 1820.
Inscribed to "F[anny]. B[rawne]. from J. K."
Bequest of Amy Lowell, 1925.
Keats *EC8.K2262.820l (F)

37. Autograph letter to George and Georgiana Keats; [Hampstead, 14–31 October 1818].
Contains " 'Tis the 'witching time of night.' "
MS Keats 1.39

38. Percy Bysshe Shelley.
Autograph letter to John Keats;
Pisa, 27 July 1820.
MS Keats 4.17.1

IX. The Exaltation of Keats

39.  *The Poetical Works of John Keats. A new edition.*
London: Edward Moxon, 1846. Inscribed: "A
Tennyson Cheltenham Feb:27. 1847 – J. T.
Fields from A Tennyson May 27th 1869" and
"This copy of Keats belonged to Tennyson
and is the Volume the Laureate carried
about in his pocket. He gave it to me in 1869,
and the writing on the opposite page is his.
James T. Fields."
Gift of Thomas Whittemore, 1950.
Keats *EC8.K2262.B846p3a (B)

40.  *The Poetical Works of John Keats.* London: By
permission of the proprietor, William Smith,
1840.
Matthew Arnold's copy, with his bookplate
and his autograph transcription of three
poems by Keats on the fly leaves.
Henry Saltonstall Howe Fund, 1962.
Keats *EC8.K2262.B840p (B)

41.  *The Poetical Works of John Keats. With a
memoir, by Richard Monckton Milnes. A new
edition.* London: Edward Moxon & Co., 1861.
Inscribed, "Isabel Swinburne from her affec^t
brother A. C. Swinburne."
Gift of Arthur A. Houghton, Jr., 1955.
Keats *EC8.K2262.B861p (D)

42.  *The Poetical Works and Other Writings of John
Keats. Now first brought together, including
poems and numerous letters not before published.
Edited with notes and appendices by Harry
Buxton Forman. . . .* London: Reeves &
Turner, 1883. 4 volumes.
Inscribed in volume 1: "To Jenny from
William Morris January 17th 1889."
Gift of Arthur A. Houghton, Jr., 1941.
Keats *EC8.K2262.C883p2 (A)

43.  *The Poetical Works of John Keats. With a life.*
Boston: Little, Brown and Company; New
York: Evans and Dickerson; Philadelphia:
Lippincott, Grambo and Co., [1855].
From the library of Ralph Waldo Emerson,
with his autograph list of references on the
back end-paper.
Deposited by the Ralph Waldo Emerson
Memorial Association, 1944.
*AC85.Em345.Zy854k

44.  *The Poetical Works of John Keats. With a
memoir, by the Rt. Hon. the Lord Houghton. A
new edition.* London: Edward Moxon & Co.,
1868.
Charles Dickens's copy, with his bookplate.
Gift of Arthur A. Houghton, Jr., 1941.
Keats *EC8.K2262.B868p (D)

45.  *The Poetical Works of John Keats. Reprinted from
the original editions with notes by Francis T.
Palgrave. . . .* London and New York:
Macmillan, 1905.
Inscribed to H. W. Eliot by T. S. Eliot, 1905.
Gift of Mrs. Henry Ware Eliot, 1954.
*AC9.El464.Zz905k

46.  *The Poetical Works of John Keats. With a
memoir, by Richard Monckton Milnes. A new
edition.* London: Edward Moxon, 1854.
Amy Lowell's copy, with her bookplate.
Bequest of Amy Lowell, 1925.
Keats *EC8.K2262.B854p (B)

47.  Benjamin Robert Haydon.
Life mask of John Keats, 1816.
Acquired with funds presented by Arthur A.
Houghton, Jr., 1972.
*71Z-3

The exhibition is supplemented with material
from the Keats Iconography Collection, formed
by Louis Arthur Holman.
Acquired with funds presented by Arthur A.
Houghton, Jr., 1940.

# The Harvard Keats Collection:
## A Short History

T HE HARVARD KEATS COLLECTION, like most of the College Library's research collections, has been built up almost entirely through private benefactions. It had small beginnings: two autograph scraps produced by the unfortunate habit of Charles Cowden Clarke and Joseph Severn of dissecting the several manuscripts left in their hands at the poet's death, for the gratification of visitors who expressed their admiration for his works or simply wished to collect autographs. Clarke cut apart an early draft of "I stood tip-toe upon a little hill," from which a slip bearing lines 38-48, 53-60, and 107-110 found its way into the album of James Thomas Fields, the Boston publisher of Ticknor & Fields fame. (It has since been joined by three similar slips from the same manuscript, all from different sources.)

Severn, who accompanied Keats to Rome and outlived him by some fifty years, drew many posthumous portraits of him (several are in the Collection) and for most of the rest of his life distributed fragments of "Isabella: or, the Pot of Basil" and "Otho the Great." A slip bearing IV.ii.128-140 and V.i.18–32 of "Otho" also found its way into the Fields album, which was given to Harvard in 1915 by the publisher's widow, Annie Adams Fields, herself a celebrated Boston hostess.[1] (Six more fragments from "Otho" and five fragments of "Isabella" later came into the Harvard collection.) The album contained many other pieces by American and British writers, most of whom were Ticknor & Fields authors and had been entertained in Mr. and Mrs. Fields's home. It was accompanied by a series of more substantial manuscripts by Dickens and others, the most celebrated of which is the holograph of Hawthorne's *The House of the Seven Gables*.

The Harvard Library had not previously been remarkable for its collection of literary manuscripts. Indeed, up to that point librarians had been reluctant to accept manuscripts of any kind, though they had acquired a number of medieval codices used as teaching aids in the classics, and several large historical archives such as those amassed by the German historian Christoph Daniel Ebeling (but his collection had been purchased mainly for its printed material), the papers of Jared Sparks and Charles Sumner, and a few others. Ten years were to elapse before the bequest of the poet Amy Lowell (1874–1925) provided the solid foundation that underpinned the Keats Collection and led to much more.

Miss Lowell was born into an affluent and distinguished Boston family, an intellectual, if conservative, milieu. Her brothers were Abbott Lawrence Lowell, who became President

---

[1] Although not herself a Keatsian, Mrs. Adams belonged to a group chronicled by Hyder E. Rollins and Stephen M. Parrish in *Keats and the Bostonians* (Cambridge, Mass., 1951). Members of this circle were responsible for bringing to New England much primary and secondary material about the poet, and several of them will appear presently in this short history.

of Harvard University in succession to Charles William Eliot, and Percival Lowell, traveller and astronomer, founder of the observatory at Flagstaff, Arizona, where he hoped to be able to verify Giovanni Schiaparelli's theory of the existence of canals (and possibly life) on Mars. Amy Lowell was educated privately and encouraged to travel widely in Europe, developing a taste for art and literature, especially poetry. At home in Brookline she had the run of the large family library, where she read extensively.

At the age of fifteen she came upon the works of John Keats and was immediately captivated; as her biographer S. Foster Damon said, Keats was "the poet predestinate to her discovery." In her late twenties she determined to make poetry her life work, and she also began to collect first editions and manuscripts of English, American, and French writers, forming an impressive library eventually bequeathed to Harvard along with the income of a trust that makes substantial additions possible. After her death and until the Houghton Library was built, her books were housed on the top floor of Widener Library, in the north-west corner next to the Woodberry Poetry Room and the Child Memorial Library. Her Keats material is now kept in the Keats Room, and in the Amy Lowell Room nearby is the bulk of her large library, notable for long runs of first editions, association copies, and manuscripts of her favorite British authors: Jane Austen, the Brontës, the Brownings, George Eliot, Sir Walter Scott, and many more.

Damon has said that her Keats collection began when she "bought all the Keats material in the Locker-Lampson sale [in 1905]." That may have been a defining moment, but in fact she started earlier. Her first important acquisition seems to have been a letter from Keats to Fanny Brawne (4 July [?] 1820; Rollins 270) at the G. I. Ellis sale in 1902. Next she acquired some twenty-five letters, most of them to the poet's publishers Taylor & Hessey, through Quaritch at the Taylor family sale in 1903, with two more at a supplementary sale the next year.

It was a year later that she swept up most of the Keats material in Frederick Locker-Lampson's famous Rowfant Library. This had been purchased *en bloc* by the American collector E. Dwight Church, who kept only selected items and disposed of most of the rest through the New York booksellers Dodd, Mead & Co. Many of the greatest collectors of the day divided the spoils. Almost all of the Keats books and manuscripts went to Amy Lowell, including seven more letters, the holographs of "The Eve of St. Agnes" and the sonnet "On First Looking into Chapman's Homer," and the second of three leaves of the final draft of "I stood tip-toe" (the first leaf was joined to it in 1947 by the Friends of the Harvard College Library, and the third and last was presented by Arthur A. Houghton, Jr., in 1951). She missed only one Keats letter in the Rowfant Library (to Joseph Severn, 1 November 1816; Rollins 9), which Locker had selected for what he called his Great Album; this, containing many important letters and manuscripts dating from the Renaissance to the late nineteenth century, was sold by Dodd, Mead to Paul M. Warburg and passed to his son-in-law, Samuel Grimson, who deposited it in the Houghton Library in 1952; his widow presented it to Harvard eight years later. It is instructive to note how the magnetism of a strong core collection attracts other significant resources.

Miss Lowell went on adding books and manuscripts whenever possible, until in 1924 she could write, "as far as I can make out, I have one of the largest, if not the largest, collection of Keats material now in existence." As she remarked, the only other private collection that might rival hers was that formed by Keats's first biographer, Richard Monckton Milnes, which had descended to the Marquess of Crewe and, as we shall see, eventually joined hers at Harvard through the generosity of Arthur Houghton. In 1921 her friend Elizabeth Ward Perkins had given her yet another great manuscript, the ode "To Autumn" that George Keats had presented to Anna Barker Ward; and her last major acquisition was the verse letter to George Keats (Margate, [1816]; Rollins 5), which she bought at the W. H. Arnold sale in 1924.

The fame of her collection was such that in 1921 she was invited to deliver the centenary lecture on Keats at Yale. While preparing her paper, she wrote to William Lyon Phelps, "I know so much about that man that I do not know what other people know and what they don't. I do not think I ever felt as though I knew any one—any historical character, I mean—as well as I know Keats. He is as clear to my senses as though he were one of the contemporary poets of today, but can I get all that into a lecture? There's no saying."[2]

Although she was untrained in the techniques of scholarship and biography, surely the idea of writing a new life of Keats had already crossed her mind. In particular she felt that earlier biographers had dealt shabbily with Fanny Brawne, dismissing her as a heartless flirt. The lecture set her off on the project that was to occupy her remaining years, work that also brought her closer to other Keatsians in New England.

They were in general lesser collectors, not having Miss Lowell's means, but not without importance. Some of the things they gathered have also come to the Houghton Library. One member of this circle was Fred Holland Day, the eccentric photographer and publisher, partner in the publishing house of Copeland & Day, who owned two letters that have since been added to the collection: one to Charles Cowden Clarke ([London, 8 or 11 November 1816]; Rollins 10), which he left to the Dedham Historical Society from whom it was purchased for Harvard by Mr. Houghton in 1974, and one to Mrs. James Wylie ([Hampstead, 24 [?] March 1820]; Rollins 253), which passed into the collection of E. Hyde Cox of Manchester, Massachusetts, and was acquired by Harvard in 1948. In Miss Lowell's view, perhaps his most important possession was a series of thirty-one letters from Fanny Brawne to Keats's sister, Fanny Keats Llanos, which went far to vindicate Miss Brawne's sincere affection and admiration for the poet. But since acquiring them in 1889, Day withheld from public view all but a few tantalizing excerpts, while continually promising an edition that never materialized; and his will contained restrictions so that they were not published until 1936, eight years

---

[2] Rollins and Parrish, p. 22.

after his death. Amy Lowell yearned to see and to quote what she rightly suspected was corroboration of her opinion of Fanny Brawne. Day, a master of procrastination, delighted to tease and torture her with a prospect that was never fulfilled.[3]

Amy Lowell found a more generous enthusiast in Louis A. Holman, for years dean of Boston print dealers, who had gathered an extensive collection of iconographic material and ephemera bearing on the life and works of Keats. He gave her free access for the illustration of her biography. The Holman Collection was purchased for Harvard in 1940 by Arthur A. Houghton, Jr., where it has proved to be a basic resource for students. Other members of the circle collected information and secondary materials that have also enriched Harvard's resources.

It was the gift of the Houghton Library building by Arthur A. Houghton, Jr. that provided the catalyst for great growth. The Keats Collection doubled in size overnight, and attracted still more gifts from many sources. Mr. Houghton had begun collecting Keats shortly after he left Harvard College in 1929, and continued vigorously when opportunity offered. By 1940, when the Houghton Library was in the planning stage, he had determined to place his Keats material there on permanent deposit, and to allow scholars access to it on the same terms that governed the use of other collections in the Harvard Library. Over a period of years he presented various segments of the deposited collection while adding still more. He completed his gift in 1971.

In an article on Arthur Houghton's private library,[4] the present writer described his Keats collection as it then stood:

> The letters and papers deposited by Mr Houghton include three
> noteworthy groups: first, the Crewe Papers, representing the collections
> made by Monckton Milnes for his work on Keats; second, the Keats-
> Haydon correspondence, an exchange of seventeen letters on either side;
> and third, the Paradinas Papers, containing the correspondence of Fanny
> Keats Llanos and the American branch of the Keats family. Besides these
> many individual pieces were acquired by Mr Houghton from various
> sources. There are holograph drafts and fragments of some eighteen
> poems, and transcripts and commonplace books (the sole authority for
> some of the texts of Keats) by Woodhouse, Brown, Haydon, Reynolds, and
> others, together with much of the great mass of material on the Keats
> Circle so ably edited by Hyder Rollins. One important Keats holograph

---

[3] He bequeathed the letters, with other primary and secondary Keatsiana, to the Hampstead Public Library for Wentworth Place. His will actually specified that they could not be published until 1961, but a loophole was provided by British copyright law; see Rollins and Parrish, pp. 49-53. Fragmentary proof sheets of his abortive edition, completed by typed transcripts prepared for him, survive in a unique set at Harvard.

[4] *The Book Collector*, Spring 1957, pp. 38-39.

was in the autograph album of Emma Isola, Lamb's adopted daughter, which also contains contributions by Wordsworth, Lamb, Hunt, Landor, and others.

Four copies of the 1817 *Poems* include presentations to Reynolds, Severn, and Wells; five of *Endymion* include Keats's own annotated copy and one he inscribed to Shelley; five of *Lamia* include a presentation to Lamb and the corrected proof-sheets, which range beside four pages of the holograph early draft and the complete finished draft as sent to the printer. Most interesting among fourteen books from Keats's library are the seven annotated volumes of his Shakespeare.

If one were to single out any item not mentioned above, it would be the great journal-letter to George and Georgiana Keats ([Hampstead], 14 February–3 May [1819]; Rollins 159), containing drafts of eleven poems. Amy Lowell's collection had included one leaf; the other twenty-eight, all now known, were given by Mr. Houghton. It might be noted, too, that among the Crewe Papers there was also a handful of manuscripts forged by the notorious Major Byron, which Monckton Milnes almost persuaded himself were genuine; they are thus permanently retired from circulation while providing a useful object-lesson for students.

Among the other gifts attracted by Mr. Houghton's creation of the Keats Room and housed there from its inception is the comprehensive collection of editions of Keats's works formed by the sculptor John Gregory, from the first collected Galignani edition to the latest, providing both an overview of the transmission of Keats's text and a gallery of publishers' bindings from the early nineteenth century to the present day. The most important accession in recent times is the extensive manuscript journal of Benjamin Robert Haydon, from which the Keats-Haydon correspondence had been extracted earlier. It was presented in 1977 by Willard B. Pope in memory of his wife , Evelyn Ryan Pope. Professor Pope edited and published the text of the journal (5 vol., 1960-63), but reproduced only a selection of Haydon's lively drawings and the many letters by other hands that are inserted in it.

Significant accessions can appear in unexpected places. Several years ago the Library began to collect modern Latin American literature in a systematic way. It became known that the most mysterious and desirable text to many scholars was yet unpublished: *Imagen de John Keats* by the Argentinian author Julio Cortázar (1914–1984). Arthur Houghton was consulted, and he encouraged the library to pursue it. "Don't pay too much for it," he cautioned. Negotiations with the Cortázar estate were protracted, so the typescript and accompanying annotated copies of Keats texts did not arrive in Cambridge until after Arthur's death. They are part of the Keats Collection today, gift in 1991 of the Friends of the Harvard College Library in honor of Arthur A. Houghton, Jr.

Since its establishment the Keats Room has been kept up to date with the latest definitive editions and other published work on Keats, so that it is and will remain a comprehensive working library for research. The printed books are listed in the Harvard College

Library catalogue. A detailed catalogue of the primary materials is here published in hard copy; it is also available through the Internet, as part of the Archive and Manuscript Finding Aids at Harvard and Radcliffe. The collection of manuscripts is unlikely to grow dramatically in future years. Barring some unexpected discovery, almost all are now in permanent collections, with the largest concentration at Harvard. We are grateful to all who chose to place these resources here, where we hope that they will be a fruitful source of scholarship for many years to come.

W. H. Bond

LIBRARIAN OF THE HOUGHTON LIBRARY, *EMERITUS*

CATALOGUE OF THE
HARVARD KEATS COLLECTION

Sed thanquam formosa vale vale inquit Heiesp ho la!.
Thou like Poetry letter - so you shall have some I was going.
to give Reynolds.

Season of Mists and mellow fruitfulness,
Close bos om friend of the maturing sun;
Conspiring with him how to load and bless
The vines with fruit that round the thatch eves run;
To bend with apples the mossd Cottage trees,
and fill all fruit with ripeness to the core;
To swell the gourd, and plump the hazle shells
With a white kernel; to set budding more,
and still more later flow ers for the bees
Untill they think warm days will never cease
For summer has o'er brimm'd their clammy Cells.

Who hath not seen thee oft amid thy stores?
Sometimes whoever seeks abroad may find
Thee sitting careless on a granary floor,
Thy hair soft-lifted by the winnowing wind;
or on a half reap'd furrow sound asleep,
Dased with the fume of poppies, while thy hook
Spares the next swath and all its twined flowers:
And sometimes like a gleaner thou dost keep
Steady thy laden head across a brook;
or by a Cyder press, with patient look,
Thou watchest the last oozings hours by hours.

JOHN KEATS. Autograph letter signed to Richard Woodhouse, 21 September 1819, including a fair copy of the ode "To Autumn" (MS Keats 1.64). Bequest of Amy Lowell.

# Introductory Note

T HERE ARE 150 "POETICAL TEXTS" by John Keats in the most recent edition of his poetry. For this corpus, 561 manuscripts are known. Only 126 of these are autograph manuscripts: poems in letters, fragments, poems copied into printed books, and a few drafts and fair copies. Of that number, 91 are in the Harvard Keats Collection, giving it the distinction of preserving almost three-quarters of Keats's extant autograph poetry.

The remainder of the surviving manuscripts are authoritative transcripts. Keats's friends, particularly Richard Woodhouse, legal advisor to Keats's publisher Taylor and Hessey, and Charles Armitage Brown, with whom Keats went on a walking tour of the Lake District and Scotland in the summer of 1818, collected and preserved his poetry both during his brief life, and following his death. As Jack Stillinger has remarked, Keats did not put a high value on his autograph manuscripts. He often gave away or discarded his working drafts. The fact that Keats read over and corrected his friends's transcripts, frequently accepting their spelling and punctuation (see MS Keats 3.1,f.86$^v$, and 3.6, p.54, for example), gives these transcripts importance in the study of the texts. Indeed, in several cases Stillinger chose such transcripts in preference to surviving fair copies by Keats as copy-text in his 1978 edition of the poems. Section II of this catalogue brings together, arranged by first line, all autograph manuscripts and transcripts in the collection. Additionally, the transcripts are described in more detail in Section III of this catalogue.

Keats's friends, notably Joseph Severn and Charles Cowden Clarke, shared his casual attitude towards his manuscripts. They cut up some of the longer manuscripts into souvenir fragments of a few lines, which they gave to friends, and to admirers of Keats's poetry. As the provenance notes in this catalogue record (see particularly "I stood tip-toe" and "Isabella; or, the Pot of Basil"), many of these fragments have been reunited at Harvard after long and tortuous travels.

Of the 251 letters by Keats that are known, 86 in his autograph are at Harvard, along with transcripts by Richard Woodhouse and John Jeffrey of another 24 letters that have not survived in the poet's hand. This makes the Harvard Keats Collection the single largest respository for Keats's letters; these are listed in Section I. These letters are joined by an extraordinarily rich assemblage of material *about* Keats, much of which has been published in *Keats Circle*; this is detailed in Section IV.

*The Poems of John Keats*, edited by Jack Stillinger, is the reference edition for the titles and first lines used throughout this catalogue. Other reference works cited are listed below. Personal names have been standardized, with cross-references from significantly different forms of the name given in the Index.

# ABBREVIATIONS USED

A          *The Poems of John Keats*, edited by Miriam Allott. 1970

G          *The Poetical Works of John Keats*, edited by H. W. Garrod, 2nd. Oxford, 1958

Hampstead  *The Poetical Works and Other Writings of John Keats*, edited by H. Buxton
           Forman, revised by Maurice Buxton Forman. 8 v. New York, 1938-39

KeJ        "John Keats," in *Index of English Literary Manuscripts. Volume IV, Part II*, edited
           by Barbara Rosenbaum. London and New York, 1990

*KC*       *The Keats Circle: Letters and Papers and More Letters and Poems of the Keats Circle*,
           edited by Hyder Edward Rollins. 2 v. 2nd ed. Cambridge, Mass., 1965

Rollins    *The Letters of John Keats, 1814-1821*, edited by Hyder Edward Rollins. 2 v.
           Cambridge, Mass., 1958

S          *The Poems of John Keats*, edited by Jack Stillinger. Cambridge, Mass., 1978

Stillinger *John Keats. Poetry Manuscripts at Harvard: A Facsimile Edition*, edited by Jack
           Stillinger; with an essay on the manuscripts by Helen Vendler. Cambridge,
           Mass., 1990

Leslie A. Morris

JUNE 1995

# I. LETTERS BY JOHN KEATS

*arranged chronologically, including transcripts where the autograph letter is not known*

**I.I**

**A.L. (unsigned) in verse, to George Keats; Margate, August [1816].**

Published as *Full many a dreary hour have I past* ("To My Brother George"). Rollins 5.

4p. on 2 conjugate leaves, 25 x 20.3 cm. Wove paper watermarked: IPING | 1813. Small piece torn from top right corner of f.1, affecting date on recto and three lines on verso. At top of p. 1, in John Jeffrey's hand: "(published)."

William Harris Arnold (sale, Anderson, 10–11 November 1924, lot 506) to Amy Lowell. Bequeathed, 1925.

**I.2**

**A.L.s. to Joseph Severn; [London, 1 November 1816].** Rollins 9.

2p. on 1 leaf, 23.4 x 18.8 cm. Laid paper, posthorn watermark.

Attested by Severn at Rome, 27 May 1879, before British vice-consul Alexander Roesler Franz, with consular seal; Frederick Locker (*The Rowfant Library*, 1886, p.208); Dodd, Mead & Co. (catalogue, *The Rowfant Autographs*, [1905?], p.37); Paul M. Warburg, ca.1908; Mr. and Mrs. Samuel Grimson. Presented by Mrs. Grimson, 1960.

**I.2.1**

**A.L.s. to Charles Cowden Clarke; [London, 8 or 11 November 1816].** Rollins 10.

2p. on 1 leaf (fragment of original leaf), 12.3 x 18.4 cm. Laid paper, posthorn watermark. On verso, fragment of address in JK's hand: "[Clerk]enwell."

F. Holland Day; Dedham (Massachusetts) Historical Society. Purchased as the gift of Arthur A. Houghton, Jr., 1974.

**I.3**

**A.L.s. to Benjamin Robert Haydon; [London], 20 November [1816].**

Contains *Great spirits now on earth are sojourning*. Rollins 11.

1p. on 1 leaf, 24.7 x 19.1 cm. Wove paper watermarked: PINE & THOMAS | 1812.

Formerly tipped in Haydon's MS. diary; passed down in the family through the hands of Frederick W. Haydon and Miss Ellen Haydon; purchased in 1932 by Maurice Buxton Forman, who removed and sold the Keats letters; offered by Scribner Book Store, New York (catalogue 132, 1946, lot 118); acquired by Arthur A. Houghton, Jr. Presented, 1952.

The Haydon diary itself was acquired in 1951 by Professor Willard Bissell Pope and presented by him in 1977. It was edited and published by Professor Pope (Cambridge, 1960-63).

Haydon transcript, 4.7.24.

**I.4**

**A.L.s. to Benjamin Robert Haydon; [London, 21 November 1816].**

Contains revised version of *Great spirits now on earth are sojourning*. Rollins 12.

3p. on 2 leaves. F.1, 16.3 x 19 cm., contains text of letter on recto, address on verso; a piece 5.5 x 11.2 cm. containing the signature was cut away and inscribed as follows: "Cut by M^rs Haydon from a letter to her husband—& handed to me by her son Fred—November 23^rd 1848 F[rancis] Bennoch." It was supposed to be sent by Bennoch to Henry Wadsworth Longfellow, but instead was attached to a watercolor portrait of Keats by Joseph Severn, from which it is now detached and restored to the original letter. F.2, 23.3 x 18.4 cm., contains the sonnet; verso blank. Laid paper, posthorn watermark.

Except as noted, same provenance as 1.3.

Haydon transcript, 4.7.24.

### 1.5
**A.L.s. to Charles Cowden Clarke; [London, 17 December 1816].** Rollins 14.

2p. on 2 conjugate leaves, 20.2 x 12.6 cm. Laid paper watermarked: [script] M & J | 1815, with fragment of countermark, probably a posthorn.

Frederick Locker (his signature, dated 1881; *The Rowfant Library*, 1886, p.208); Dodd, Mead & Co.; purchased by Amy Lowell, 1905. Bequeathed, 1925.

### 3.3, p.49
**Woodhouse transcript; to John Hamilton Reynolds, 9 March 1817.**
Rollins 16. Original not known.

### 3.3, p.42
**Woodhouse transcript; to John Hamilton Reynolds, 17 March 1817.**
Rollins 18. Original not known.

Patmore transcript, 3.10(22).

### 1.6
**A.L.s. to Taylor and Hessey; [London, 12 or 13 April 1817].** Rollins 20.

2p. on 2 conjugate leaves, 11.2 x 9.4 cm. Wove paper watermarked: BASTED [MILL] | 18[ ].

Family of John Taylor (sale, Sotheby, 8–9 June 1903, lot 541) to Bernard Quaritch; purchased by Amy Lowell, 1904. Bequeathed, 1925.

### 3.3, p.43
**Woodhouse transcript; to John Hamilton Reynolds, 17–18 April 1817.**
Rollins 22. Original not known.

Patmore transcript, 3.10(23).

### 1.7
**A.L.s. to Benjamin Robert Haydon; Margate, [10–11 May 1817].** Rollins 26.

4p. on 2 conjugate leaves, 24.8 x 20 cm. Wove paper watermarked: JOHN HAYES | 1814. Annotated in Haydon's hand on p.1: "I wonder if they will be. B R Haydon," referring to Keats's words, "I pray God that our brazen Tombs be nigh neighbours."

Same provenance as 1.3.

Haydon transcript, 4.7.24.

### 1.8
**A.L.s. to Taylor & Hessey; Margate, 16 May [1817].** Rollins 27.

3p. on 2 conjugate leaves, 25 x 20.2 cm. Same paper as 1.7.

Same provenance as 1.6 (lot 542 in sale, 1903).

Woodhouse transcript, 3.3, p.100.

### 1.9
**A.L.s. to Taylor and Hessey; [London, 10 June 1817].** Rollins 28.

3p. on 2 conjugate leaves, 18.6 x 11.3 cm. Wove paper unwatermarked.

Same provenance as 1.6 (lot 543 in sale, 1903).

Woodhouse transcript, 3.3, p.101.

### 1.10
**A.L.s. to Jane and Mariane Reynolds; Oxford, [4 September 1817].** Rollins 30.

2p. on 1 leaf, 25 x 20 cm. Wove paper unwatermarked. 7 lines written by Benjamin Bailey at the top of p.1 heavily scratched out and illegible. Sealed with cameo portrait of John Milton in black wax.

James R. Osgood (William E. Benjamin, catalogue 4, March 1886, p.15); C. W. Frederickson (sale, Bangs, 24 May 1897, lot 2277); John Harvey Vincent Arnold (sale, Anderson, 19 April 1904, lot 595); Dodd, Mead & Co.

(catalogue 78, November 1905, lot 106); A. S. W. Rosenbach. Presented by Arthur A. Houghton, Jr., 1952.

Woodhouse transcript, 3.3, p.74.

## I.II

**A.L.s. to Jane and Mariane Reynolds; Oxford, [14 September 1817].** Rollins 34.

4p. on two conjugate leaves, 25 x 20 cm. Wove paper watermarked: 1810. Profile seal of bearded man in helmet, red wax.

Same provenance as 1.6 (lot 553 in sale, 1903).

Woodhouse transcript, 3.3, p.19.

## 3.3, p.46
**Woodhouse transcript; to John Hamilton Reynolds, 21 September 1817.**
Rollins 36. Original not known.

## I.I2

**A.L.s. to Benjamin Robert Haydon; Oxford, 28 September [1817].** Rollins 37.

3p. on 2 conjugate leaves, 22.2 x 17.9 cm. Wove paper watermarked: FELLOWS | 1812. Sealed with cameo portrait of William Shakespeare, red wax.

Same provenance as 1.3.

Haydon transcript, 4.7.24.

## I.I3

**A.L.s. to Benjamin Bailey; Hampstead, [8] October [1817].** Rollins 38.

4p. on 2 conjugate leaves, 24.8 x 20 cm. Wove paper watermarked: J BUDGEN | 1814.

Same provenance as 1.6 (lot 532 in sale, 1903).

Woodhouse transcript, 3.3, p.76; Patmore transcript, 3.10(25).

## I.I4

**A.L.s. to Benjamin Bailey; [London, 28–30 October 1817].**
Contains a version of *A thing of beauty is a joy forever* ("Endymion") IV.1–29. Rollins 39.

4p. on 2 leaves, in part crossed, 22.4 x 18.7 cm. Wove paper watermarked: J WHATMAN | W BALSTON & Cº | 1814. Seal as in 1.12.

Part of the collection formed by Richard Monckton Milnes, 1st baron Houghton; descended with other Keatsiana to Robert Offley Ashburton Crewe-Milnes, Lord Crewe, from whom the whole collection was acquired in 1945 by Arthur A. Houghton, Jr. Presented, 1952.

## I.I5

**A.L.s. to Benjamin Bailey; [London, 3 November 1817].**
Contains a version of *A thing of beauty is a joy forever* ("Endymion") IV.146–181. Rollins 41.

4p. on 2 leaves, in part crossed, 22.4 x 18.5 cm. Same paper as 1.14. Seal as in 1.12.

F.1 was owned by H. J. Severingham Bailey (sale, Anderson, 25 November 1927, lot 77) to Robert G. Murphy; presented by Mrs. Murphy in memory of Ray Livingston Murphy, 1953. F.1, same provenance as 1.6 (lot 540 in sale, 1903).

Woodhouse transcript, 3.3, p.79.

## I.I6

**A.L.s. to Benjamin Bailey; [Dorking, 22 November 1817].** Rollins 43.

6p. on 1 leaf and 2 conjugate leaves, 2 pages crossed, 23 x 18.8 cm. Wove paper watermarked: C WILMOTT | 1816. Seal as in 1.11, black wax.

Same provenance as 1.6 (lot 538 in sale, 1903).

Woodhouse transcript, 3.3, p.80.

**3.3, p.50**
**Woodhouse transcript; to John Hamilton Reynolds, 22 November 1817.**
Rollins 44. Original not known.

**3.9, f.5ʳ**
**Jeffrey transcript; to George and Tom Keats, 21–27[?] December 1817.**
Rollins 45. Original not known.

**1.17**
**A.L.(unsigned) to callers on John Taylor; [London, January 1818?].** Rollins 47.

2p. on 2 conjugate leaves, 18.6 x 11.4 cm. Wove paper unwatermarked.

Same provenance as 1.6 (lot 557 in sale, 1903).

Woodhouse transcript, 3.3, p.102.

**3.3, p.2**
**Woodhouse transcript; to John Taylor, 10 January 1818.**
Rollins 49. Original not known.

Transcript by unidentified hand, 3.10(29).

**1.18**
**A.L.s. to Benjamin Robert Haydon; [London, 10 January 1818].** Rollins 50.

3p. on 2 conjugate leaves, 25.4 x 20.3 cm. Laid paper watermarked: C CRIPPS | 1814. Seal as in 1.11, black wax.

Same provenance as 1.3.

**3.9, f.2ᵛ**
**Jeffrey transcript; to George and Tom Keats, 13–19 January 1818.**
Rollins 52. Original not known.

**1.19**
**A.L.s. to John Taylor; [London], 23 [January 1818].** Rollins 54.

2p. on 2 conjugate leaves, 25.4 x 20.2 cm. Laid paper watermarked with fleur-de-lys and date, 1814.

Sold at auction by Bangs (11 January 1897, lot 193) to William Harris Arnold (sale, Anderson, 10-11 November 1924, lot 507) to Miss Edith Reynolds, who bequeathed it to the Osterhout Free Public Library, Wilkes-Barre, Pennsylvania. Presented by Arthur A. Houghton, Jr., 1965.

Woodhouse transcript, 3.3, p.102; transcript by unidentified hand, 3.10(29).

**1.20**
**A.L.s. to Benjamin Bailey; [London], 23 January [1818].** Rollins 55.

4p. on 2 conjugate leaves, 25.4 x 20.4 cm. Same paper as 1.18. Seal as in 1.12, black wax.

Same provenance as 1.6 (lot 533 in sale, 1903).

Woodhouse transcript, 3.3, p.83.

**3.9, f.3ᵛ**
**Jeffrey transcript; to George and Tom Keats, 23–24 January 1818.**
Rollins 56. Original not known.

**3.3, p.53**
**Woodhouse transcript; to John Hamilton Reynolds, 31 January 1818.**
Rollins 58. Original not known.

**3.3, p.28 and p.55**
**Woodhouse transcripts (2); to John Hamilton Reynolds, 3 February 1818.**
Rollins 59. Original not known.

**1.21**
**A.L.s. to John Taylor;**
[London, 5 February 1818]. Rollins 60.

2p. on 2 conjugate leaves, 22.7 x 18.6 cm. Wove paper watermarked: GATER| 1815. Seal as in 1.11, black wax.

Same provenance as 1.6 (lot 544 in sale, 1903).

Woodhouse transcript, 3.3, p.103.

**3.9, f.5ᵛ**
**Jeffrey transcript; to George and Tom Keats, 14[?] February 1818.**
Rollins 61. Original not known.

**1.22**
**A.L.s. to George and Tom Keats;**
**Hampstead, [21 February 1818].** Rollins 64.

4p. on 2 conjugate leaves, 25.8 x 20.4 cm. Laid paper watermarked with fleur-de-lys. Red wax seal, design indistinguishable. At top of p.1 in John Jeffrey's hand: "copied July 1845."

Acquired by Arthur A. Houghton, Jr., 1951. Presented, 1970.

Jeffrey transcript, 3.9, f.1ʳ.

**1.23**
**A.L.s. to Benjamin Bailey;**
**Teignmouth, [13 March 1818].**
Contains *Four seasons fill the measure of the year.* Rollins 67.

4p. on 2 conjugate leaves, in part crossed, 23.3 x 18.8 cm. Wove paper watermarked: M & J LAY| 1817. Seal as in 1.11.

Same provenance as 1.6 (lot 537 in sale, 1903).

Woodhouse transcript, 3.3, p.95.

**3.3, p.56**
**Woodhouse transcript; to John Hamilton Reynolds, 14 March 1818.**
Rollins 68. Original not known.

**1.24**
**A.L.s. to Benjamin Robert Haydon;**
**Teignmouth, [21 March 1818].**
Contains *For there's Bishop's Teign* and *Where be ye going, you Devon maid.* Rollins 70.

4p. on 2 conjugate leaves, 22.6 x 18.8 cm. Wove paper watermarked: HAGAR & Cᵒ | 1817. Red wax seal, design indistinguishable.

Same provenance as 1.3.

Transcript by unknown hand in Keats *EC8.K2262. W848ma v.I.

**1.25**
**A.L.s. to James Rice;**
**Teignmouth, [24 March 1818].**
Contains *Over the hill and over the dale.* Rollins 72.

4p. on 2 conjugate leaves, 22.7 x 18.6 cm. Wove paper unwatermarked. Red wax seal, mostly cut away.

Same provenance as 1.6 (lot 554 in sale, 1903).

Woodhouse transcript, 3.3, p.III.

**3.3, p.74**
**Woodhouse transcript; to John Hamilton Reynolds, 25 March 1818.**
Rollins 74. Prose portion only. Original not known.

**1.26**
**A.L.s. to Benjamin Robert Haydon;**
**[Teignmouth, 8 April 1818].** Rollins 75.

4p. on 2 conjugate leaves, 23 x 18.5 cm. Wove paper unwatermarked. Red wax seal, mostly cut away.

Same provenance as 1.3.

**3.3, p.58**
**Woodhouse transcript; to John Hamilton Reynolds, 9 April 1818.**
Rollins 76. Original not known.

**I.27**
**A.L.s. to John Hamilton Reynolds;**
**[Teignmouth, 17 April 1818].**
Rollins 77, where it is wrongly dated 10 April.

2p. on 1 leaf, 23.1 x 18.5 cm. Wove paper unwatermarked.

Acquired by Arthur A. Houghton, Jr., 1941. Presented, 1970.

Woodhouse transcript, 3.3, p.61.

**3.3, p.62**
**Woodhouse transcript; to John Hamilton Reynolds, 27 April 1818.**
Rollins 79. Original not known.

**3.3, p.64**
**Woodhouse transcript; to John Hamilton Reynolds, 3 May 1818.**
Rollins 80. Original not known.

**I.28**
**A.L.s. to Benjamin Bailey; Hampstead,**
**[21, 25 May 1818].** Rollins 83.

4p. on 2 conjugate leaves, 22.7 x 18.8 cm. Wove paper watermarked: JOHN HAYES | 1815. Seal as in I.11.

Same provenance as I.6 (lot 534 in sale, 1903).

Woodhouse transcript, 3.3, p.86.

**I.29**
**A.L.s. to Marian and Sarah Jeffrey;**
**Hampstead, 4 June [1818].** Rollins 84.

4p. on 2 conjugate leaves, 23.2 x 18.8 cm. Wove paper unwatermarked.

Adrian H. Joline (sale, Anderson, 19 October 1915, lot 420); Anson Conger Goodyear (sale, Anderson, 1-2 February 1927, lot 255) to A. S. W. Rosenbach. Presented by Arthur A. Houghton, Jr., 1952.

**I.30**
**A.L.s. to Benjamin Bailey;**
**London, [10 June 1818].** Rollins 86.

4p. on 2 conjugate leaves, 23.3 x 18.8 cm. Wove paper watermarked: RUSE & TURNERS | 1817.

Same provenance as I.6 (lot 535 in sale, 1903).

Woodhouse transcript, 3.3, p.88.

**I.31**
**A.L.s. (John O'Grote) to John Taylor;**
**[Hampstead, 21 June 1818].** Rollins 88.

4p. on 2 conjugate leaves, 20.4 x 16.1 cm. Laid paper watermarked: J BUDGEN | 1817. Page 3 contains only the words, "M^rs Reynolds with J. K.'s respects," which were intended to be cut off and pasted into a copy of *Endymion: A Poetic Romance* (1818) for presentation.

Same provenance as I.6 (lot 545 in sale, 1903).

Woodhouse transcript, 3.3, p.9.

**I.32**
**A.L.s. to George [and Georgiana] Keats;**
**"foot of Helvellyn," 27[–28] June 1818.**
Contains *Give me your patience, sister, while I frame* ("Acrostic") and *Sweet, sweet is the greeting of eyes*. Rollins 92.

4p. on 2 conjugate leaves, 32.9 x 20.4 cm. Laid paper watermarked: J BUDGEN | 1816, with countermark of crowned lion in oval escutcheon. Seal cut away with some loss of text.

Bequeathed by Amy Lowell, 1925.

**3.9, f.6^r**
**Jeffrey transcript; to Tom Keats,**
**29 June–2 July 1818.**
Rollins 93. Original not known.

1.33
**A.L.s. to Tom Keats;**
**Auchencairn, 3–[9] July [1818].**
Contains *Old Meg she was a gipsey.* Rollins 95.

4p. on 2 conjugate leaves, 32.9 x 20.4 cm. Same paper as 1.32. Seal removed with loss of a few letters.

Given by George Keats to James Freeman Clarke. Presented by the Clarke family, 1946.

Jeffrey transcript, 3.9, f.7ᵛ.

3.3, p.71
**Woodhouse transcript; to John Hamilton Reynolds, 11, 13 July 1818.**
Rollins 96. Original not known.

1.34
**A.L.s. to Benjamin Bailey;**
**Inverary, 18–[22] July [1818].**
Contains *There is a joy in footing slow across a silent plain* ("Lines Written in the Highlands After a Visit to Burns's Country"). Rollins 99.

4p. on 2 conjugate leaves, in part crossed, 33.7 x 21 cm. Laid paper watermarked with script H and date 1817, with countermark of seated Britannia in an oval. Seal removed with loss of a few letters.

Same provenance as 1.6 (lot 536 in sale, 1903).

Woodhouse transcript, 3.3, p.90.

1.35
**A.L.s. to Tom Keats;**
**Dun an Cullen, [23–26 July 1818].**
Contains *Not Aladdin magian* ("On Visiting Staffa"). Rollins 100.

4p. on 2 leaves, formerly conjugate, 33.7 x 21 cm. Same paper as 1.34.

Same provenance as 1.14. Presented by Arthur A. Houghton, Jr., 1952.

Jeffrey transcript, 3.9, f.9ʳ.

1.36
**A.L.s. to Tom Keats; Letter Findlay,**
**3 August [1818].**
Contains *Upon my life, Sir Nevis, I am piqu'd* and *Read me a lesson, Muse, and speak it loud.* Rollins 101.

4p. on 2 conjugate leaves, in part crossed, 32.7 x 20.2 cm. Laid paper watermarked: D & A CAMPBELL | 1817, with countermark of seated Britannia in an oval. Wafers removed affecting a few letters.

H. Buxton Forman; Maurice Buxton Forman (sale, Sotheby, 6 May 1936, lot 817) to A. S. W. Rosenbach. Presented by Arthur A. Houghton, Jr., 1952.

3.9, f.12ʳ
**Jeffrey transcript; to Mrs. James Wylie,**
**6 August 1818.**
Rollins 102. Original not known.

1.37
**A.L.s. to Jane Reynolds;**
**[Hampstead], 1 September [1818].** Rollins 106.

2p. on 2 conjugate leaves, part of the second torn away without loss of text, 22.9 x 18.6 cm. Wove paper watermarked: W TURNER & S[ON].

Same provenance as 1.5.

3.3, p.18
**Woodhouse transcript; to John Hamilton Reynolds, 22[?] September 1818.**
Rollins 108. Original not known.

3.3, p.13
**Woodhouse transcript; to J. A. Hessey,**
**8 October 1818.**
Rollins 110. Original not known.

1.38
**A.L.s. to Richard Woodhouse;**
**[Hampstead, 7 October 1818].** Rollins 118.

4p. on 2 conjugate leaves, 22.6 x 18.1 cm. Wove

paper watermarked: IVY MILL | 1816. Red wax seal, design indistinguishable.

Family of John Taylor (sale, Sotheby, 18-19 July 1904, lot 130) to Amy Lowell. Bequeathed, 1925.

Woodhouse transcript, 3.3, p.15.

### 1.39
**A.L.s. to George and Georgiana Keats; [Hampstead, 14–31 October 1818].**
Contains 'Tis the "witching time of night." Rollins 120.

16p. on 4 pairs of conjugate leaves; the first three pairs 24.2 x 18.8 cm. Wove paper watermarked: JOHN HAYES | 1815. The last pair 32.3 x 20.2 cm. Laid paper watermarked: W TURNER & SON, with countermark of seated Britannia in an oval.

Same provenance as 1.14. Presented by Arthur A. Houghton, Jr., 1952.

Jeffrey transcript, 3.9, p.13ʳ.

### 1.40
**A.L.s. to James Rice; [Hampstead], 24 November [1818]. Rollins 122.**

3p. on 2 conjugate leaves, 20.2 x 16.2 cm. Same paper as last conjugate pair of 1.39.

Same provenance as 1.6 (lot 555 in sale, 1903).

Woodhouse transcript, 3.3, p.113.

### 1.41
**A.L.(signature cut away) to Richard Woodhouse; [Hampstead, 18 December 1818]. Rollins 128.**

2p. on 2 conjugate leaves, 23 x 18.4 cm. Wove paper watermarked: FELLOWS | 1817; all edges gilt. Remains of black wax seal.

Same provenance as 1.34 (lot 131 in sale, 1904).

Woodhouse transcript, 3.3, p.27.

### 1.42
**A.L.s. to Benjamin Robert Haydon; [Hampstead, 20 December 1818].**
Rollins 130.

1p. on 1 leaf, 22.6 x 18.5 cm. Wove paper unwatermarked.

Same provenance as 1.3.

### 1.43
**A.L.s. to Benjamin Robert Haydon; [Hampstead, 20 December 1818].**
Rollins 131.

4p. on 2 conjugate leaves, 22.9 x 18.4 cm. Same paper as 1.41.

Same provenance as 1.3.

### 1.44
**A.L.s. to John Taylor; [Hampstead, 24 December 1818].**
Rollins 133.

2p. on 2 conjugate leaves, 22.9 x 18.4 cm. Same paper as 1.41. Remains of black wax seal.

Same provenance as 1.6 (lot 546 in sale, 1903).

Woodhouse transcript, 3.3, p.103.

### 1.45
**A.L.s. to George and Georgiana Keats; [Hampstead, 16 December 1818–4 January 1819].**
Contains Ever let the Fancy roam ("Fancy"); Bards of passion and of mirth ("Ode"); and I had a dove, and the sweet dove died ("Song").
Rollins 137.

12p. on 3 pairs of conjugate leaves, 40.7 x 25.3 cm. Wove paper unwatermarked.

Same provenance as 1.14. Presented by Arthur A. Houghton, Jr., 1952.

Jeffrey transcript, 3.9, f.16ʳ.

**1.46**

**A.L.s. to Benjamin Robert Haydon;
[Hampstead, 2 January 1819].**
Rollins 138.

1p. on 1 leaf, 18.6 x 11.1 cm. Wove paper
unwatermarked.

Same provenance as 1.3.

**1.47**

**A.L.s. to Benjamin Robert Haydon;
[Hampstead, 10 [?] January 1819].**
Rollins 140.

2p. on 1 leaf, 22.7 x 18.6 cm. Wove paper
unwatermarked.

Same provenance as 1.3.

Haydon transcript, 4.7.24.

**1.48**

**A.L.s. to William Mayor;
[Hampstead, 4 February 1819].**
Rollins 144.

3p. on 2 conjugate leaves, 18.5 x 11.3 cm. Wove
paper unwatermarked. Remains of black wax
seal.

Maggs Brothers catalogue 600 (1934), item 132. Pre-
sented by Arthur A. Houghton, Jr., 1952.

**1.49**

**A.L.s. to Benjamin Robert Haydon;
[Hampstead, 18 [?] February 1819].**
Rollins 146.

2p. on 2 conjugate leaves, 22.7 x 18.6 cm.; piece
12.6 x 4 cm. torn from address leaf, not
affecting text. Wove paper unwatermarked.
Remains of black wax seal.

Same provenance as 1.3.

**4.7.24**

**Haydon transcript; to Benjamin Robert
Haydon, 8 March 1819.**
Rollins 149. Original not known.

**1.50**

**A.L.s. to Joseph Severn;
[Hampstead, 29 March 1819].** Rollins 153.

3p. on 2 conjugate leaves, 18.5 x 11.2 cm. Wove
paper unwatermarked. Remains of black wax
seal. On p.2, signed affidavit of genuineness by
Severn, witnessed by Alexander Roesler Franz,
British vice-consul at Rome, 27 May 1879.

Same provenance as 1.5.

**1.51**

**A.L. (signature cut away) to Benjamin
Robert Haydon; [Hampstead, 13 April 1819].**
Rollins 157.

4p. on 2 conjugate leaves, 22.3 x 18.6 cm.; an
irregular piece, about 13 x 10 cm., cut from
second leaf, containing the signature on the
recto and part of the address and postmarks on
the verso. Wove paper unwatermarked.
Remains of black wax seal. Annotated by
Haydon, "To Lady Grahm[?] I gave auto-."

Same provenance as 1.3.

**1.52**

**A.L.s. to Fanny Keats;
[Hampstead, 1 May [?] 1819].**
Contains *Two or three posies*. Rollins 158.

4p. on 2 leaves, formerly conjugate, 22.3 x 18.6
cm. Same paper as 1.51. Black wax seal with
lyre and motto, "QUE ME NEGLIGE ME
DESOLE."

Given by Fanny Keats to Frederick Locker, with his
signature on p.4; thereafter, same provenance as 1.5.

Unidentified transcript, 5.2.1(458).

**1.53**

**A.L. (last leaf with signature lacking) to George and Georgiana Keats;**
**[Hampstead], 14 February–3 May [1819].**
Contains *Why did I laugh tonight?*; *When they were come unto the Faery's court*; *He was to weet a melancholy carle* ("Character of C.B."); *As Hermes once took to his feathers light* ("On a Dream"); *O what can ail thee, knight at arms* ("La Belle Dame sans Merci"); *Happy, happy glowing fire* ("Song of Four Fairies"); *Fame, like a wayward girl, will still be coy* ("On Fame"); *How fever'd is the man who cannot look* ("On Fame"); *O soft embalmer of the still midnight* ("Sonnet to Sleep"); *O Goddess! hear these tuneless numbers, wrung* ("Ode to Psyche"); and *If by dull rhymes our English must be chain'd* (first 4 lines only). Rollins 159.

58p. on 29 leaves; leaves 1-2 and 3-4 evidently former conjugate pairs, 22.6 x 18.5 cm., wove paper unwatermarked. Leaves 5-29 evidently single leaves when written, 20.3 x 12.8 cm., wove paper watermarked: RUSE & TURNER | 1817, with leaves 5-11 and 20-27 bearing the first half of the watermark and leaves 12-19, 28-29 the latter half. (An examination and attempt to match watermarks shows that it is unlikely if not impossible for these leaves to have been conjugate pairs when written.)

Leaves 1-2, William Harris Arnold (sale, Anderson, 10-11 November 1924, lot 508) to Howard Sachs. Presented by Arthur A. Houghton, Jr., 1970. Leaves 3-8, 10-29, same provenance as 1.14; presented by Arthur A. Houghton, Jr., 1970. Leaf 9, William Harris Arnold (lot 509 in sale, 1924) to Amy Lowell. Bequeathed, 1925.

Jeffrey transcript; sole available source of end of letter, 3.9, f.20ʳ.

**1.54**

**A.L.s. to Sarah Jeffrey;**
**Hampstead, [31 May 1819]. Rollins 164.**

4p. on 2 conjugate leaves, 22.4 x 18.7 cm. Wove paper unwatermarked. Remains of black wax seal. Silked.

Edward Sandford Burgess (sale, American Art Association, 16-17 December 1929, lot 104) to A. S. W. Rosenbach. Presented by Arthur A. Houghton, Jr., 1952.

**1.55**

**A.L.s. to Benjamin Robert Haydon;**
**[Hampstead, 17 June 1819].**
Rollins 170.

3p. on 2 conjugate leaves, 22.6 x 18.7 cm. Same paper as 1.54. Remains of red wax seal.

Same provenance as 1.3.

**3.3, p.30**

**Woodhouse transcript; to John Hamilton Reynolds, 11 July 1819.**
Rollins 175. Original not known.

**1.56**

**A.L.s. to Richard Abbey;**
**Shanklin, [16 July 1819]. Rollins 177.**

2p. on 2 conjugate leaves, 24.1 x 19.4 cm., an oblong (blank?) portion 24.1 x 15 cm. lacking from leaf 2, an irregular piece about 12 x 11 cm. torn from leaf 1, affecting a large part of the text. Wove paper watermarked: [C WIL]MOTT | [1]818. Remains of red wax seal.

Presented by Dr. Harris Kennedy, 1943.

**1.57**

**A.L.s. to Fanny Brawne;**
**[Shanklin, 25 July 1819]. Rollins 178.**

4p. on 2 conjugate leaves, 24.7 x 20 cm. Same paper as 1.56. Remains of red wax seal.

Sotheby sale, 2 March 1885, lot 3; Templeton Crocker; John Howell, bookseller. Presented by Arthur A. Houghton, Jr., 1969.

### 1.58
**A.L.s. (last half only) to Benjamin Bailey; [Winchester, 14 August 1819].** Rollins 181.

2p. on 1 leaf, 24.8 x 20 cm. Same paper as 1.56. Remains of red wax seal.

Same provenance as 1.6.

Woodhouse transcript, 3.3, p.99.

### 1.59
**A.L.s. to Fanny Brawne; Winchester, 17 [i.e. 16] August [1819].** Rollins 182.

4p. on 2 conjugate leaves, 24.7 x 20 cm. Same paper as 1.56. Seal cut away.

Sotheby sale, 2 March 1885, lot 5; R. H. Toedteberg (sale, Anderson, 14 October 1904, lot 394) to Amy Lowell. Bequeathed, 1925.

### 1.60
**A.L.s. to John Taylor; Winchester, 24 August [1819].** Rollins 183.

4p. on 2 conjugate leaves, 24.9 x 20.5 cm. Page 4 contains A.L.s. from Charles Armitage Brown to Taylor (Rollins 184). Wove paper watermarked: J GREEN | 1815. Remains of red wax seal.

Same provenance as 1.6 (lot 547 in sale, 1903).

Woodhouse transcripts, 3.3, p.32 and 4.20.6.

### 1.61
**A.L.s. to John Taylor; Winchester, 1 September [1819].** Rollins 188.

3p. on 2 conjugate leaves, 24.9 x 20.4 cm. Same paper as 1.60. Seal as in 1.12.

Same provenance as 1.6 (lot 548 in sale, 1903).

Woodhouse transcripts, 3.3, p.38 and 4.20.7.

### 1.62
**A.L.s. to J. A. Hessey; Winchester, 5 September [1819].** Rollins 189.

2p. on 2 conjugate leaves, 24.9 x 20.4 cm. Same paper as 1.60. Remains of red wax seal.

Same provenance as 1.6 (lot 549 in sale, 1903).

Woodhouse transcript, 4.20.7.

### 1.63
**A.L.s. to John Taylor; Winchester, 5 September [1819].**
Contains *Upon a time, before the faery broods* ("Lamia") II.122–162, plus 15 cancelled lines. Rollins 190.

4p. on 2 conjugate leaves, in part crossed, 24.9 x 20.4 cm. Same paper as 1.60. Remains of red wax seal.

Same provenance as 1.6 (lot 550 in sale, 1903).

Woodhouse transcript, 3.3, p.39.

### 3.3, p.33
**Woodhouse transcript; to John Hamilton Reynolds, 21 September 1819.**
Rollins 193. Original not known.

### 1.64
**A.L.s. to Richard Woodhouse; [Winchester, 21 September 1819].**
Contains *Season of mists and mellow fruitfulness* ("To Autumn") and *Fanatics have their dreams, wherewith they weave* ("The Fall of Hyperion") I.1–11, I.61–86, II.1–4, II.6. Rollins 194.

8p. on 2 pairs of conjugate leaves, 24.7 x 20.1 cm. Same paper as 1.56. Remains of red wax seal.

Same provenance as 1.6 (lot 552 in sale, 1903).

### 4.3.27, f.17
**Brown transcript; to Charles Armitage Brown, 22 September 1819.**
Rollins 195. Original not known.

4.3.27, f.19
**Brown transcript; to Charles Armitage
Brown, 23 September 1819.**
Rollins 197. Original not known.

**1.65**
**A.L.s. to Benjamin Robert Haydon;
Winchester, [3 October 1819].**
Includes a short A.L.s. to Haydon from Charles
Armitage Brown. Rollins 201.

4p. on 2 conjugate leaves, 24 x 19.4 cm. Wove
paper watermarked: J Green | 1818. Red wax
seal torn off, affecting several lines of text.

Same provenance as 1.3.

**1.66**
**A.L.s. to Fanny Brawne;
[Winchester, 11 October 1819].**
Rollins 202.

3p. on 2 conjugate leaves, 23.2 x 18.5 cm. Laid
paper watermarked with posthorn in crowned
escutcheon and date 1807. Red wax seal, design
indistinguishable.

Sotheby sale, 2 March 1885, lot 7; Sotheby, 11 April
1919, lot 787 ("the property of a lady") to Maggs Broth-
ers; Frank B. Bemis; A. S. W. Rosenbach. Presented
by Arthur A. Houghton, Jr., 1952.

**1.67**
**A.L.s. to Fanny Brawne;
[Winchester, 19 October 1819].**
Rollins 204.

2p. on 2 conjugate leaves, 23.7 x 18.7 cm. Laid
paper watermarked with fleur-de-lys in
crowned escutcheon and script initials J A.
Remains of red wax seal.

Sotheby sale, 2 March 1885, lot 9; John A. Spoor (sale,
Parke-Bernet, 26–28 April 1939, lot 461). Presented by
Arthur A. Houghton, Jr., 1951.

**1.68**
**A.L.s. to Joseph Severn;
[Hampstead, 10 November 1819].** Rollins 207.

3p. on 2 conjugate leaves, 20.1 x 12.2 cm. Same
paper as 1.56. Small red wax seal, design
indistinguishable. Watercolor sketch of man's
head, and test streaks of various tints, on
address leaf, probably by Severn.

Same provenance as 1.5.

**1.69**
**A.L.s. to Joseph Severn;
[Hampstead, 15 November 1819].** Rollins 209.

2p. on 1 leaf, 20.3 x 12.4 cm. Wove paper
unwatermarked. Pen sketch by Severn on p.2.

Same provenance as 1.5.

**1.70**
**A.L.s. to James Rice;
[Hampstead, December 1819].** Rollins 212.

4p. on 2 conjugate leaves, 19 x 12.4 cm. Same
paper as 1.56.

Same provenance as 1.6 (lot 556 in sale, 1903).

Woodhouse transcript, 3.3, p.108.

**1.71**
**A.L.s. to Fanny Brawne;
[Hampstead, 10 [?] February 1820].**
Rollins 221.

3p. on 2 conjugate leaves, 18.9 x 11.2 cm. Wove
paper unwatermarked. Remains of red wax
seal.

Sotheby sale, 2 March 1885, lot 11; Alfred Morrison
(sale, Sotheby, 19 April 1918, lot 1712, and 6 May 1919,
lot 2926); Frank B. Bemis; A. S. W. Rosenbach. Pre-
sented by Arthur A. Houghton, Jr., 1952.

**1.72**

**A.L.s. to Fanny Brawne;**
**[Hampstead, February [?] 1820]. Rollins 225.**

4p. on 2 conjugate leaves, 18.6 x 11.2 cm. Wove paper unwatermarked.

Sotheby sale, 2 March 1885, lot 13; F. S. Ellis (sale, Sotheby, 16 November 1885, lot 1846). Presented by Lucius Wilmerding, 1942.

**1.73**

**A.L.s. to Fanny Brawne;**
**[Hampstead, February [?] 1820]. Rollins 226.**

3p. on 2 conjugate leaves, 18.7 x 12.6 cm. Laid paper, fragment of unidentified watermark. Remains of red wax seal.

Sotheby sale, 2 March 1885, lot 14; F. S. Ellis (sale, Sotheby, 10 November 1885, lot 1847); Alfred Morrison (sale, Sotheby, 19 April 1918, lot 1711, and 6 May 1919, lot 2925); Frank B. Bemis; A. S. W. Rosenbach. Presented by Arthur A. Houghton, Jr., 1952.

**1.74**

**A.L.s. to James Rice; [Hampstead,**
**14–16 February 1820]. Rollins 228.**

4p. on 2 conjugate leaves, 22.6 x 18.9 cm. Wove paper unwatermarked, embossed: BATH and crown. Seal removed with loss of one letter on p. 3.

John Boyd Thacher (sale, Anderson, 3 November 1915, lot 607); George L. Clawson (sale, Anderson, 29 November 1920, lot 257); Frank B. Bemis; A. S. W. Rosenbach. Presented by Arthur A. Houghton, Jr., 1952.

Woodhouse transcript, 3.3, p.106; transcript by unidentified hand, 3.10(27).

**1.75**

**A.L.s. to Fanny Brawne;**
**[Hampstead, February 1820]. Rollins 230.**

4p. on 2 conjugate leaves, 18.9 x 11.2 cm. Wove paper unwatermarked, embossed: BATH and crown. Remains of red wax seal.

Sotheby sale, 2 March 1885, lot 16; F. S. Ellis (sale, Sotheby, 16 November 1885, lot 1849). Presented by Lucius Wilmerding, 1942.

**1.76**

**A.L.s. to Fanny Brawne;**
**[Hampstead, 29 [?] February 1820].**
Rollins 238.

3p. on 2 leaves, formerly conjugate, 18.7 x 11.2 cm. Wove paper unwatermarked, embossed: BATH and crown.

Sotheby sale, 2 March 1885, lot 20; F. S. Ellis (sale, Sotheby, 16 November 1885, lot 1852); William A. Read (sale, American Art Association, 8-9 January 1936, lot 213). Presented by Arthur A. Houghton, Jr., 1952.

**1.77**

**A.L.s. to Fanny Brawne;**
**[Hampstead, March [?] 1820]. Rollins 247.**

4p. on 2 conjugate leaves, 15.2 x 9.8 cm. Laid paper watermarked: [    ] | & | ALLFORD | 1817. Remains of red wax seal.

Sotheby sale, 2 March 1885, lot 26; F. S. Ellis (sale, Sotheby, 16 November 1885, lot 1857). Presented by Lucius Wilmerding, 1942.

Both the English and the American editions of *Letters of John Keats to Fanny Brawne* (1878) include a rather crude facsimile of this letter, tipped in as an illustration.

**1.78**

**A.L. (signature cut away) to Mrs. James**
**Wylie; [Hampstead, 24 [?] March 1820].**
Completed by attaching a cut signature plus a few words from another letter. Rollins 253.

4p. on 2 conjugate leaves, 22.5 x 18.3 cm. Wove paper unwatermarked, embossed: BATH and crown. Remains of red wax seal.

Lewis J. Cist (sale, Bangs, 5-8 October 1886, lot 2855); F. Holland Day; Edward Hyde Cox. Purchased by Harvard, 1948.

**4.3.27, f.25**
**Brown transcript; to Charles Armitage Brown, 15 May 1820.**
Rollins 260. Original not known.

Patmore transcript, made from the Brown transcript, 3.10(20).

**1.79**
**A.L.s. to Fanny Brawne;**
**[Kentish Town, June [?] 1820].** Rollins 262.

4p. on 2 conjugate leaves, in part crossed, 20.6 x 12.6 cm. Laid paper watermarked with fleur-de-lys. Red wax seal.

Not in the sale of 2 March 1885; early provenance not traced. Bequeathed by Amy Lowell, 1925.

**1.80**
**A.L.s. to John Taylor;**
**[Kentish Town, 11 [?] June 1820].**
Contains revisions for *St. Agnes' Eve—Ah, bitter chill it was* ("The Eve of St. Agnes").
Rollins 263.

3p. on 2 conjugate leaves, 22.4 x 18.5 cm. Wove paper watermarked: FELLOWS | 1815. Red wax seal torn away.

Same provenance as 1.6 (lot 551 in sale, 1903).

Woodhouse transcript, 3.3, p.105.

**4.3.27, f.25**
**Brown transcript; to Charles Armitage Brown, ca. 21 June 1920.**
Rollins 266. Original not known.

**1.81**
**A.L. (signature cut away) to Fanny Brawne;**
**[Kentish Town, June [?] 1820].** Rollins 268.

2p. on 2 conjugate leaves, 20.5 x 12.6 cm. Laid paper watermarked with fleur-de-lys. Red wax seal, sprig of myrtle with motto, "SOLO LIBERO."

Sotheby sale, 2 March 1885, lot 32; F. S. Ellis (sale,

Sotheby, 16 November 1885, lot 1862). Presented by Arthur A. Houghton, Jr., 1952.

**1.82**
**A.L.s. to Fanny Brawne;**
**[Kentish Town, 4 July [?] 1820].** Rollins 270.

2p. on 2 conjugate leaves, 20.8 x 12.9 cm. Laid paper watermarked with fleur-de-lys and date 1819. Remains of wafer.

Sotheby sale, 2 March 1885, lot 33; F. S. Ellis (sale, Sotheby, 16 November 1885, lot 1864); Ellis & Elvey, booksellers (*General catalogue*, [1895], no. 465); Gilbert I. Ellis (sale, Sotheby, 28 October 1902, lot 205) to Amy Lowell. Bequeathed, 1925.

**1.83**
**A.L.s. to Benjamin Robert Haydon;**
**[Hampstead, 14 August [?] 1820].**
Rollins 283.

1p. on 1 leaf, 18 x 11.2 cm. Wove paper watermarked: [ ]HOMAS | [18]16.

Same provenance as 1.3.

**4.3.27, f.27**
**Brown transcript; to Charles Armitage Brown, 14 August 1820.**
Rollins 284. Original not known.

**1.84**
**A.L.s. to Benjamin Robert Haydon;**
**[Hampstead, August [?] 1820].** Rollins 287.

2p. on 2 conjugate leaves, 19.9 x 12.6 cm. Laid paper watermarked with fleur-de-lys.

Dodd, Mead & Co. (catalogue 55, December 1899, no.203); Harry Bache Smith (*A Sentimental Library*, 1914, no. 235); Frank B. Bemis; A. S. W. Rosenbach. Presented by Arthur A. Houghton, Jr., 1952.

**4.3.27, f.28**
**Brown transcript; to Charles Armitage Brown, August[?] 1820.**
Rollins 288. Original not known.

**1.85**
**A.L.s. to Benjamin Robert Haydon;**
**Hampstead, [August [?] 1820].**
Rollins 289.

1p. on 1 leaf, 18.5 x 11.3 cm. Wove paper watermarked: Simm[  ] | 181[  ].

Same provenance as 1.3.

Haydon transcript, 4.7.24.

**1.86**
**A.L.s. to William Haslam;**
**[Hampstead, 23 August 1820].** Rollins 291.

3p. on 2 conjugate leaves, 18.3 x 11.3 cm. Wove paper unwatermarked. Remains of red wax wafer.

Rowland Eyles Egerton-Warburton; Lady Ashbrook (sale, Sotheby, 16 March 1937, lot 497); A. S. W. Rosenbach; sold privately by John F. fleming. Presented by Arthur A. Houghton, Jr., 1967.

**1.87**
**A.L.s. to Charles Armitage Brown;**
**off Yarmouth, Isle of Wight,**
**28 September [1820].** Rollins 302.

4p. on 2 conjugate leaves, 22.5 x 18.4 cm. Wove paper unwatermarked. Red wax seal covered with paper.

Same provenance as 1.5.

Brown transcript, 4.3.27, f.30.

**4.3.27, f.32**
**Brown transcript; to Charles Armitage Brown, 1 November 1820.**
Rollins 306. Original not known.

**4.3.27, f.30**
**Brown transcript; to Charles Armitage Brown, 30 November 1820.**
Rollins 310. Original not known.

Season of Mist and mellow fruitfulness.
Close bosom friend of the maturing sun;
Conspiring with him how to load and bless
The Vines with fruit that round the thatch eves run
To bend with apples the mossd Cottage trees
And fill all fruits with ripeness to the core
To swell the gourd, and plump the hazle shells
With a white kernel; to set budding more
And still more, later flowers for the bees
Until they think warm days with never cease
For Summer has o'er brimm'd their clammy cells—

Who hath not seen thee? ~~for thy haunts are many~~
Sometimes whoever seeks ~~for thee~~ abroad may find
Thee sitting ~~careless~~ on a granary floor
Thy hair soft lifted by the winnowing wind
~~While bright the sun slants through the barn;~~
~~on on a half reap'd furrow sound asleep~~
~~Or sound asleep in a half reap'd field~~
Dos'd with red poppies; while thy reaping hook
~~Spares from some slumbrous warm slumbers creep~~
Or on a half reap'd furrow sound asleep
Dos'd with the fume of poppies, while thy hook
~~Spares the next swath, and all its fumed flowers~~
~~Spares for some slumbrous minutes the next swath;~~

And sometime like a gleaner thou dost keep
Steady thy laden head across the brook;
Or by a Cyder-press with patient look
Thou watchest the last oozing hours by hours

JOHN KEATS. "To Autumn." Autograph manuscript, draft (MS Keats 2.27). Bequest of Amy Lowell.

# II. POETRY

*arranged by first line*

*A thing of beauty is a joy forever*
("Endymion") G.65; A.116; S.102.

**1.14**      A.MS. of IV.1-29, in letter to
Benjamin Bailey, 28–30 October 1817. KeJ 64.
Rollins 39.

**1.15**      A.MS. of IV.146-181, in letter to
Benjamin Bailey, 3 November 1817. KeJ 66.
Rollins 41.

**3.2, f.329ᵛ**  Woodhouse transcript of Keats's
alterations in the text.

**3.3, p.3**      I.777-781 in Woodhouse transcript of
letter to John Taylor, 30 January 1818. Rollins
57.

**3.3, p.4**      Revisions in Woodhouse transcript
of letter to John Taylor, 27 February 1818.
Rollins 65.

**3.3, p.7**      Proof revisions in Woodhouse
transcript of letter to John Taylor, 24 April 1818.
Rollins 78.

**3.3, p.50**      IV.581-590 in Woodhouse transcript
of letter to J. H. Reynolds, 22 November 1817.
KeJ 67. Rollins 44.

*After dark vapours have oppress'd our plains*
G.458; A.101; S.89.

**3.1, f.14ʳ**   Woodhouse transcript. KeJ 10.

**3.2, f.18ʳ**   Woodhouse transcript. KeJ 9.

**3.10(12)**   Patmore transcript. KeJ 14.

**4.20.9**   Woodhouse transcript. KeJ 12.

**4.20.10**   Woodhouse transcript. KeJ 13.

*Ah! who can e'er forget so fair a being*
(stanza 3 of *Woman! when I behold thee. . .*)
G.27; A.47; S.40.

**3.12, f.28ʳ**   Stephens transcript.

*Ah! woe is me! poor Silver-wing!*
("Faery Song") G.437; A.490; S.297.

**3.6, p.61**   Brown transcript. KeJ 16.

*All gentle folks who owe a grudge*
G.560; A.366; S.273.

**3.10(26)**   Transcript, unidentified hand.
KeJ 18.

*And what is Love?—It is a doll dress'd up*
("Modern Love") G.499; A.393; S.288.

**3.2, f.75ʳ**   Woodhouse transcript. KeJ 19.

*As from the darkening gloom a silver dove*
G.531; A.8; S.31.

**3.1, f.13ᵛ**   Woodhouse transcript. KeJ 24.

**3.2, f.8ʳ**   Woodhouse transcript. KeJ 22.

**3.10(16)**   Patmore transcript. KeJ 26.

**4.20.9**   Woodhouse transcript. KeJ 25.

*As Hermes once took to his feathers light*
("On a Dream") G.471; A.498; S.326.

**1.53**        A.MS. in letter to George and
Georgiana Keats, 14 February–3 May 1819.
KeJ 28. Rollins 159.

**3.1, f.78ʳ**   Woodhouse transcript. KeJ 32.

**3.2, f.71ʳ**   Woodhouse transcript. KeJ 30.

**3.6, p.56**   Brown transcript. KeJ 29.

**3.9, f.26ʳ**   Jeffrey transcript. KeJ 34.

**3.10(19)**   Payne transcript. KeJ 35.

*As late I rambled in the happy fields*
("To a Friend Who Sent Me Some Roses")
G.41; A.46; S.54.

**3.5, p.20**   Tom Keats transcript. KeJ 460.

**3.12, f.45ʳ**   Stephens transcript.

*Bards of passion and of mirth*
("Ode")        G.268; A.446; S.294.

**1.45**        A.MS. in letter to George and
Georgiana Keats, 16 December 1818–4 January
1819. KeJ 37. Rollins 137.

**3.1, f.71ʳ**   Woodhouse transcript. KeJ 40.

**3.2, f.69ʳ**   Woodhouse transcript. KeJ 39.

**3.6, p.22**   Brown transcript. KeJ 38.

*Before he went to live with owls and bats*
("Nebuchadnezzar's Dream")
G.533; A.288; S.98.

**3.6, p.62**   Brown transcript. KeJ 42.

**3.12, f.69ᵛ**   Stephens transcript. KeJ 43.

*Blue!—'Tis the life of heaven—the domain*
("Answer to a Sonnet. . .") G.464; A.309; S.234.

**3.1, f.17ᵛ**   Woodhouse transcript. KeJ 47.

**3.2, f.23ʳ**   Woodhouse transcript. KeJ 45.

**3.10(9)**   Patmore transcript. KeJ 50.

**4.20.9**   Woodhouse transcript. KeJ 49.

**4.20.10**   Woodhouse transcript. KeJ 51.

*Bright star, would I were stedfast as thou art*
G.475; A.736; S.327.

**3.6, p. 60**   Brown transcript. KeJ 53.

*Byron, how sweetly sad thy melody*
("To Lord Byron") G.477; A.9; S.31.

**3.2, f.217ʳ**   Woodhouse transcript. KeJ 493.

**4.20.9**   Woodhouse transcript. KeJ 494.

*Cat! who hast past thy grand climacteric*
("To Mrs. Reynolds's Cat") G.534; A.292; S.222.

**3.1, f.16ʳ**   Woodhouse transcript. KeJ 497.

**3.2, f.24ʳ**   Woodhouse transcript. KeJ 496.

*Chief of organic numbers!*
("Lines on Seeing a Lock of Milton's Hair")
G.479; A.292; S.223.

**1.20**        A.MS., in letter to Benjamin Bailey,
23 January 1818. KeJ 228. Rollins 55.

**2.15.1**      A.MS., draft with revisions, of lines
1-17; written on f.13ᵛ of a manuscript otherwise
containing autograph drafts of prose and
poetry by Leigh Hunt; no other autograph
material of Keats elsewhere in the MS. 49p. on
40 leaves, 18.7 x 13.7 cm. Bluish laid paper
watermarked: J A | F, with countermark of a
bell. Bound in tan morocco by Tout. KeJ 226.
Stillinger, pp.60-61.

H. Buxton Forman (sale, Anderson, 15 March 1920,
lot 347) to Amy Lowell. Bequeathed, 1925.

This MS. with 2.15.2 contains the complete text of Keats's poem.

Works by Leigh Hunt, all in heavily revised drafts, are: f.1ʳ-11ʳ, "Hero and Leander," lines 98-293 (end); f.13ʳ-18ʳ, translation of Theocritus, Idyll XI, "The Cyclops;" f.19ʳ-21ʳ, translation of Theocritus, Idyll XII, "The Lover;" f.23ʳ-24ʳ, unidentified poem, probably a translation, beginning *Jove's daughters & the Poets have this task*; f.25ʳ-33ʳ, translation of Theocritus, Idyll VII, "The Rural Journey;" f.34ʳ, poem beginning *Shakespeare, the sprightliest, gravest, gentlest, wisest*; f.34ʳ-36ʳ, poem beginning *Godiva, fair and young, royally drest*, differing from the poem of that title published in 1850.

**2.15.2**      A.MS., draft with revisions, comprising lines 18 to end. 2p. on 1 leaf, 18.6 x 11.4 cm. Laid paper watermarked: BATH (within curved line). Verso also contains quotations in Hunt's hand from *King John* and *Twelfth Night*. KeJ 226. Stillinger, pp. 61-65.

Presented by Arthur A. Houghton, Jr., 1970.

**3.1, f.80ʳ**      Woodhouse transcript. KeJ 232.

**3.2, f.155ʳ**      Woodhouse transcript. KeJ 231.

**3.6, p.46**      Brown transcript. KeJ 229.

---

### Come hither all sweet maidens, soberly
("On a Leander Which Miss Reynolds, My Kind Friend, Gave Me") G.535; A.107; S.94.

**2.12**      A.MS. signed, draft with revisions. 1p. on 1 leaf, 19.2 x 15.9 cm. Wove paper unwatermarked. On verso, in unidentified hand, is the text of Wordsworth's "Lines Written When Sailing in a Boat at Evening." KeJ 307. Stillinger, pp. 54-55.

Sale, Sotheby, 9 June 1920, lot 106 ("the property of a lady") to W. T. Spencer; Frank B. Bemis, sold privately through A. S. W. Rosenbach. Presented by Arthur A. Houghton, Jr., 1970.

**3.2, f.193ʳ**      Woodhouse transcript. KeJ 308.

**3.12, f.66ʳ**      Stephens transcript.

**4.20.9**      Woodhouse transcript. KeJ 309.

---

### Dear Reynolds, as last night I lay in bed
("To J. H. Reynolds, Esq.") G.484; A.320; S.241.

**3.2, f.65ʳ**      Woodhouse transcript. KeJ 60.

---

### Deep in the shady sadness of a vale
("Hyperion: A Fragment") G.276; A.394; S.329.

**3.1, f.22ʳ**      Woodhouse transcript. KeJ 145.

**3.2, f.79ʳ**      Woodhouse transcript. KeJ 144.

---

### Ever let the Fancy roam
("Fancy") G.264; A.441; S.290.

**1.45**      A.MS. in letter to George and Georgiana Keats, 16 December 1818–4 January 1819. KeJ 91. Rollins 137.

**3.2, f.183ʳ**      Woodhouse transcript. KeJ 94.

**3.6, p.15**      Brown transcript. KeJ 92.

---

### Fair Isabel, poor simple Isabel!
("Isabella; or, The Pot of Basil") G.215; A.326; S.245.

**2.17.1**      A.MS., fragment of early draft, comprising lines 49-56, 65-72, and the first line of a cancelled stanza. 2p. on 1 leaf, cut from a larger sheet; 6.6 x 20.5 cm. Laid paper unwatermarked. KeJ 181. Stillinger, pp.70-71.

Joseph Severn; sale, Sotheby, 28 July 1930, lot 220; Alfred Meyer (sale, American Art Association, 12-13 January 1938, lot 143). Presented by Arthur A. Houghton, Jr., 1945.

**2.17.2**     A.MS., fragment of early draft, comprising lines 89-96 and 113-120 (last line defective). 2p. on 1 leaf, cut from a larger sheet; 7.4 x 17 cm. Laid paper unwatermarked. KeJ 184. Stillinger, pp. 72-73.

Joseph Severn; C. Salaman; Blanche H. Dupuy, tipped in a copy of *Lamia*, 1820 (sale, Anderson, 18 January 1922, lot 199); John A. Spoor (sale, Parke-Bernet, 26-28 April 1939, lot 464). Presented by Arthur A. Houghton, Jr., 1946.

**2.17.3**     A.MS., fragment of early draft, comprising lines 233-248 and 257-320. 4p. on 2 leaves, 15.7 x 19.9 cm. and 24.7 x 19.8 cm. Laid paper watermarked with script H and date 1816. KeJ 187. Stillinger, pp. 74-81.

Joseph Severn; Jerome Kern (sale, Anderson, 21-24 January 1929, lot 752) to A. S. W. Rosenbach. Presented by Arthur A. Houghton, Jr., 1945.

**2.17.4**     A.MS., fragment of early draft, comprising lines 321-326 and 345-352. 2p. on 1 leaf, cut from a larger sheet; 8.5 x 20.4 cm. Laid paper unwatermarked. KeJ 188. Stillinger, pp. 82-83.

Joseph Severn; Robert Spence; sale, Christie, 1 July 1970, lot 118. Presented by Arthur A. Houghton, Jr., 1970.

**2.17.5**     A.MS., fragment of early draft, comprising lines 417-424 and 433-472. 2p. on 1 leaf, 22.6 x 18.5 cm. Wove paper unwatermarked. KeJ 192. Stillinger, pp. 84-87.

Joseph Severn; said to have been in a Red Cross benefit sale (4 April 1916, lot unknown). Bequeathed by Amy Lowell, 1925.

**3.1, f.86ʳ**     Woodhouse transcript, revised at seven points in the autograph of John Keats. KeJ 199.

**3.2, f.30ʳ**     Woodhouse transcript. KeJ 198.

**3.3, p.62**     Woodhouse transcript. KeJ 200.

*Fame, like a wayward girl, will still be coy*
("On Fame") G.468; A.512; S.366.

**1.53**     A.MS. in letter to George and Georgiana Keats, 14 February–3 May 1819. KeJ 311. Rollins 159.

**3.1, f.80ʳ**     Woodhouse transcript. KeJ 315.

**3.2, f.152ʳ**     Woodhouse transcript. KeJ 313.

**3.6, p.49**     Brown transcript. KeJ 312.

**3.10(19)**     Payne transcript. KeJ 316.

*Fanatics have their dreams, wherewith they weave*
("The Fall of Hyperion") G.509; A.655; S.478.

**1.64**     A.MS. of I.1-11, 61-86; II.1-4, 6, in letter to Richard Woodhouse, 21 September 1819. KeJ 87. Rollins 194.

**3.2, f.165ʳ**     Woodhouse transcript. KeJ 88.

**4.20.8**     Woodhouse transcript. KeJ 89.

*Fill for me a brimming bowl*
G.540; A.6; S.30.

**3.2, f.222ʳ**     Woodhouse transcript. KeJ 98.

**4.20.9**     Woodhouse transcript. KeJ 99.

*For there's Bishop's Teign*
G.555; A.316; S.238.

**1.24**     A.MS. in letter to Benjamin Robert Haydon, 21 March 1818. KeJ 100. Rollins 70.

**Keats \*EC8.K2262.W848ma (B) v.1**
Transcript by unknown hand in v.1 of *Life, Letters, and Literary Remains of John Keats* (London, 1848).

Same hand as 3.10.27 to 30.

*Forgive me, Haydon, that I cannot speak*
("To Haydon with a Sonnet Written on Seeing the Elgin Marbles") G.478; A.105; S.93.

**Keats \*EC8.K2262.817p (G), p.122**
A.MS., fair copy. Written in the copy of *Poems* (1817) presented to John Hamilton Reynolds. KeJ 478. Stillinger, pp.48-49.

John Hamilton Reynolds; Dr. E. Horner (whose father purchased it in Leipzig c.1875); Robert Offley Ashburton Crewe-Milnes, Lord Crewe; A. S. W. Rosenbach; Frank B. Bemis. Presented by Arthur A. Houghton, Jr., 1950.

**3.2, f.22ʳ**   Woodhouse transcript. KeJ 480.

**4.7.20**   Haydon transcript.

**4.20.10**   Woodhouse transcript. KeJ 482.

*Four seasons fill the measure of the year*
G.536; A.312; S.238.

**1.23**   A.MS. in letter to Benjamin Bailey, 13 March 1818. KeJ 101. Rollins 67.

**3.2, f.215ʳ**   Woodhouse transcript. KeJ 102.

**3.3, p.98**   In Woodhouse transcript of letter to Benjamin Bailey, 13 March 1818. KeJ 103. Rollins 67.

**3.10(17)**   Patmore transcript. KeJ 105.

**3.12, f.66ᵛ**   Stephens transcript.

**4.20.9**   Woodhouse transcript. KeJ 104.

*Fresh morning gusts have blown away all fear*
("To a Young Lady Who Sent Me a Laurel Crown") G.457; A.108; S.89.

**3.1, f.15ᵛ**   Woodhouse transcript. KeJ 463.

**3.2, f.19ʳ**   Woodhouse transcript. KeJ 462.

**3.10(8)**   Patmore transcript. KeJ 465.

**4.20.9**   Woodhouse transcript. KeJ 464.

*Full many a dreary hour have I past*
("To My Brother George") G.31; A.48; S.56.

**1.1**   A.MS., draft varying slightly from version in *Poems*, 1817. KeJ 498. Rollins 5.

**3.4, f.15ʳ**   Georgiana Keats transcript, lines 1-31 only. KeJ 500.

**3.4, f.33ʳ**   George Keats transcript. KeJ 499.

**3.12, f.33ʳ**   Stephens transcript.

*Give me a golden pen, and let me lean*
("On Leaving Some Friends at an Early Hour") G.46; A.64; S.65.

**3.12, f.48ᵛ**   Stephens transcript.

*Give me women, wine, and snuff*
G.554; S.47.

**4.13.7**   Transcript in unidentified hand. KeJ 108.

*Give me your patience, sister, while I frame*
("Acrostic") G.567; A.354; S.265.

**1.32**   A.MS. in letter to George and Georgiana Keats, 27–28 June 1818. KeJ 109. Rollins 92.

*Glory and loveliness have passed away*
("To Leigh Hunt, Esq.") G.2; A.102; S.92.

**3.12, f.3ʳ**   Stephens transcript.

*God of the golden bow*
("Ode to Apollo") G.430; A.110; S.91.

**2.13**    A.MS., draft with revisions. 2p. on 1 leaf, 19.2 x 15.2 cm. Laid paper, fragment of post-horn watermark and script initials G E [?]. KeJ 111. Stillinger, pp. 50-53.

George Keats; James Freeman Clarke. Presented by the Clarke family, 1950.

**3.1, f.20ᵛ**    Woodhouse transcript. KeJ 115.

**3.2, f.14ʳ**    Woodhouse transcript. KeJ 114.

**4.20.10**    Woodhouse transcript. KeJ 117.

*God of the meridian!*
 G.482; A.300 (lines 17-41); S.227.

**3.1, f.8ʳ**    Woodhouse transcript, lines 13-25 only (29-41 in Allott). KeJ 120.

**3.2, f.56ʳ**    Woodhouse transcript. KeJ 119.

**3.3, p.54**    In Woodhouse transcript of letter to J. H. Reynolds, 31 January 1818. KeJ 118. Rollins 58.

*Good Kosciusko, thy great name alone*
("To Kosciusko") G.50; A.99; S.68.

**3.12, f.50ᵛ**    Stephens transcript.

*Great spirits now on earth are sojourning*
("Addressed to the Same"; "To Haydon") G.48; A.67; S.67.

**1.3**    A.MS., early draft in letter to Benjamin Robert Haydon, 20 November 1816. KeJ 3. Rollins 11.

**1.4**    A.MS., second draft in letter to Benjamin Robert Haydon, 21 November 1816. KeJ 4. Rollins 12.

**2.7**    A.MS., fair copy with a few corrections, probably that sent to the press. 1p. on 1 leaf, 19.4 x 12.9 cm. Laid paper, fragment of crown watermark. Dated by Keats at foot, "Christ Day"; numbered 14 at head (the number it bears in *Poems*, 1817). KeJ 5. Stillinger, pp. 20-21.

Charles Ollier [?]; A. S. W. Rosenbach. Presented by Arthur A. Houghton, Jr., 1970.

**3.5, p.17**    Tom Keats transcript. KeJ 6.

**3.12, f.49ᵛ**    Stephens transcript.

*Had I a man's fair form, then might my sighs*
("To ★ ★ ★ ★ ★ ★") G.40; A.32; S.44.

**3.5, p.15**    Tom Keats transcript. KeJ 123.

**3.12, f.43ᵛ**    Stephens transcript.

*Hadst thou liv'd in days of old*
("To ★ ★ ★ ★"; "To Mary Frogley") G.21; A.29; S.44.

**3.1, f.11ᵛ**    Woodhouse transcript. KeJ 128.

**3.2, f.223ʳ**    Woodhouse transcript. KeJ 127.

**3.12, f.21ᵛ**    Stephens transcript.

*Happy, happy glowing fire*
("Song of Four Fairies") G.443; A.506; S.359.

**1.53**    A.MS. in letter to George and Georgiana Keats, 14 February–3 May 1819. KeJ 393. Rollins 159.

**2.23**    A.MS., fair copy with a few revisions. 4p. on 4 leaves (two conjugate pairs) with early foliation 8-12 in unidentified hand, 30.4 x 19.5 cm. Laid paper watermarked: GILLING | & | ALLFORD | 1817, with countermark of a seated Britannia in a crowned oval. KeJ 394. Stillinger, pp. 132-139.

Same provenance as 1.6 (lot 559 in sale, 1903).

**3.2, f.161ʳ**   Woodhouse transcript. KeJ 396.

**3.6, p.11**   Brown transcript. KeJ 395.

### *Happy is England! I could be content*
G.50; A.100; S.55.

**2.11**   A.MS., fair copy. 1p. on 1 leaf, 18.5 x 11.4 cm. Wove paper watermarked: LA[   ] | [script] KE [   ] | 18[   ]. KeJ 129. Stillinger, pp. 6-7.

D. C. Higgs to William Carew Hazlitt, 5 December 1875; formerly tipped in *The Poetical Works of John Keats*, 1854 (now Keats *EC8.K2262.B854p2 (C)), given to Hazlitt's mother by Edward Moxon. Presented by Arthur A. Houghton, Jr., 1970.

**3.12, f.51ʳ**   Stephens transcript.

### *Hast thou from the caves of Golconda, a gem*
("On Receiving a Curious Shell, and a Copy of Verses, from the Same Ladies") G.19; A.19; S.37.

**2.1**   A.MS., fair copy. 2p. on 1 leaf, 23.8 x 18.1 cm. Laid paper watermarked: 1813. Dated at end by Keats: 1815. KeJ 328. Stillinger, pp. 2-5.

Benjamin Robert Haydon (numbered "6 F" in upper left corner, placing it in the sequence of letters once tipped in Haydon's journal); Helen Selina Blackwood (who sat for Haydon in 1833), inscribed on verso, "John Keats at 16 given to Mrs Blackwood 1833 by his Friend"; Frank Sykes (sale, Sotheby, 23 June 1947, lot 220B); Maurice Buxton Forman; in Sotheby sale, 21 May 1968, lot 383. Presented by Arthur A. Houghton, Jr., 1968.

**3.4, f.22ʳ**   Georgiana Keats transcript, lines 1-12 only. KeJ 330.

**3.4, f.36ʳ**   George Keats transcript. KeJ 329.

**3.5, p.10**   Tom Keats transcript. KeJ 331.

**3.12, f.19ᵛ**   Stephens transcript.

### *He was to weet a melancholy carle*
("Character of C[harles] B[rown]") G.498; A.496; S.326.

**1.53**   A.MS. in letter to George and Georgiana Keats, 14 February–3 May 1819. KeJ 56. Rollins 159.

**3.2, f.150ʳ**   Woodhouse transcript. KeJ 58.

**3.6, p.41**   Brown transcript. KeJ 57.

**3.9, f.25ᵛ**   Jeffrey transcript. KeJ 59.

### *Hearken, thou craggy ocean pyramid*
("To Ailsa Rock") G.491; A.364; S.272.

**3.12, f.67ʳ**   Stephens transcript.

### *Hence burgundy, claret, and port*
("Song") G.481; A.299 (lines 1-16); S.227.

**3.2, f.56ʳ**   Woodhouse transcript. KeJ 132.

**3.3, p.54**   In Woodhouse transcript of letter to John Hamilton Reynolds, 31 January 1818. KeJ 131. Rollins 58.

**3.6, p.5**   Brown transcript. KeJ 130.

### *Highmindedness, a jealousy for good*
("Addressed to Haydon") G.47; A.66; S.66.

**3.10(1)**   Unidentified transcript. KeJ 1.

**3.12, f.49ʳ**   Stephens transcript.

### *How fever'd is the man who cannot look*
("On Fame") G.469; A.513; S.367.

**1.53**   A.MS. in letter to George and Georgiana Keats, 14 February–3 May 1819. KeJ 317. Rollins 159.

**3.2, f.153ʳ**   Woodhouse transcript. KeJ 319.

**3.6, p.51**   Brown transcript. KeJ 318.

*How many bards gild the lapses of time*
G.41; A.59; S.63.

**3.12, f.44ᵛ**    Stephens transcript.


*Hush, hush, tread softly, hush, hush, my dear*
("Song") G.434; A.448; S.296.

**2.20**    A.MS., draft, with revisions. 1p. on
1 leaf, 22.5 x 18 cm. Wove paper watermarked:
IVY MILL | 1816. KeJ 136. Stillinger, pp. 92-93.

Same provenance as 1.14. Presented by Arthur A.
Houghton, Jr., 1970.

**3.2, f.131ʳ**    Woodhouse transcript. KeJ 140.

**3.6, p.27**    Milnes transcript, lines 21-24 only.
KeJ 138.

**3.6, p.28**    Brown transcript, lines 1-20 only.


*I cry your mercy—pity—love!—aye, love*
G.474; A.689; S.492.

**3.6, p.58**    Brown transcript. KeJ 148.


*I had a dove, and the sweet dove died*
("Song") G.435; A.448; S.296.

**1.45**    A.MS. in letter to George and
Georgiana Keats, 16 December 1818–4 January
1819. KeJ 149. Rollins 137.

**3.2, f.187ʳ**    Woodhouse transcript. KeJ 150.

**3.10(3)**    Milnes transcript. KeJ 151.


*I stood tip-toe upon a little hill*
G.3; A.85; S.79.

**2.8.1**    A.MS., fragment of first draft, lines
1-6, 19-23. 2p. on 1 leaf, slip cut from a larger
sheet; 6.7 x 12.4 cm. Wove paper
unwatermarked. KeJ 152. Stillinger, pp. 24-27.

Charles Cowden Clarke, authenticated in his hand at
head of recto. Presented by Miss Mildred Kennedy,
1960.

**2.8.2**    A.MS., fragment of first draft, lines
7-10, 24-27. 2p. on 1 leaf, slip cut from a larger
sheet; 3 x 12.4 cm. Wove paper unwatermarked.
KeJ 152. Stillinger, pp. 24-27.

Charles Cowden Clarke, a portion of his authentica-
tion remaining in left margin; pasted on a larger sheet
inscribed: "John Keats's Manuscript. Charles Cowden
Clarke. Villa Novello, Genoa, Dec.ʳ 28.ᵗʰ 1868"; W. H.
Doeg; Senator George Frisbie Hoar. Presented by
Mrs. Frances Foster, 1961.

**2.8.3**    A.MS., fragment of first draft, lines
38-48, 53-60, 107-110 (the last two groups of lines
here written without a break); the recto
showing in the left margin line-endings
apparently of 29-30, 32-33. 2p. on 1 leaf, cut from
a larger sheet; 11 x 12.4 cm. Wove paper
unwatermarked. KeJ 154. Stillinger, pp. 28-29.

Charles Cowden Clarke, authenticated in his hand in
left margin of recto; Leigh Hunt, removed from his
copy of *The Poetical Works of Coleridge, Shelley, and Keats*
(1819) now Keats *EC8.K2262.B819pa (B); Thornton
Leigh Hunt; James T. Fields. Presented by Mrs. James
T. Fields, 1915.

**2.8.4**    A.MS., fragment of first draft, lines
111-112, plus a cancelled version of 113-114 (recto)
and 61-64 (verso). 2p. on 1 leaf, slip cut from a
larger sheet; 4 x 11.8 cm. Wove paper, fragment
of watermark: [ ] J. KeJ 155. Stillinger, pp. 30-31.

Charles Cowden Clarke, endorsed on recto in uni-
dentified hand: "(M.S.)Keats given to me by C. C.
Clarke Esq.ʳᵉ M. M. H. Jan. 1832"; in Edwin H.
Denham catalogue XII, 1902, no. 93; Edward Sandford
Burgess. Presented by Arthur A. Houghton, Jr., 1970.

**2.5**    A.MS., draft, of lines 231-235 only;
on verso of A.MS. of *Small, busy flames play
through the fresh laid coals; q.v.* for details.
KeJ 163. Stillinger, pp. 30-31.

**2.9**      A.MS., complete fair copy. 6p. on 3 leaves (formerly one conjugate pair and a single leaf), 25 x 20.2 cm. Laid paper watermarked with triple plume on a coronet, and: MOLINEUX & JOHNSTON. Leaf 1 contains 1-96; 2, 97-182; 3, 183-242. KeJ 165. Stillinger, pp. 32-43.

Leaf 1, erased and partly legible authentication, evidently by Benjamin Robert Haydon; H. Buxton Forman; Ross Whistler. Purchased with contributions from the Friends of the Harvard College Library, 1947.

Leaf 2, authenticated by Haydon in ink on verso; Frederick Locker, 1878 (*The Rowfant Catalogue*, 1886, p.208); sold privately through Dodd, Mead & Co. to Amy Lowell in 1905. Bequeathed, 1925.

Leaf 3, inscribed in ink on verso: "a Fragment of Dear Keats poetry & writing, given to me by him & by me to Miss Barrett [Elizabeth Barrett Browning] December 30th 1842. B. R. Haydon"; H. P. Moulton-Barrett (sale, Sotheby, 7 June 1937, lot 40) to A. S. W. Rosenbach. Presented by Arthur A. Houghton, Jr., 1951.

**3.8**      Tom Keats transcript. KeJ 166.

**3.10(2)**   Prideaux transcript; lines 61-64, 111-114 only, plus four cancelled lines. KeJ 156.

**3.12, f.4$^r$**   Stephens transcript.

### If by dull rhymes our English must be chain'd
G.472; A.521; S.368.

**1.53**      A.MS. of lines 1-4 only in letter to George and Georgiana Keats, 14 February–3 May 1819. KeJ 167. Rollins 159.

**3.1, f.80$^r$**   Woodhouse transcript. KeJ 172.

**3.2, f.154$^r$**   Woodhouse transcript. KeJ 170.

**3.6, p.55**   Brown transcript. KeJ 169.

**3.9, f.27$^r$**   Jeffrey transcript. KeJ 173.

### If shame can on a soldier's vein-swoll'n front
("King Stephen") G.385; A.690; S.496.

**2.28**      A.MS., draft with revisions, of I.ii.19b - iv.58. 7p. on 5 leaves, 38.9 x 23.1 cm., except the last leaf, 32.7 x 23.5 cm. Wove paper watermarked: J Green | 1818. KeJ 208. Stillinger, pp. 232-245.

Same provenance as 1.14. Presented by Arthur A. Houghton, Jr., 1970.

This MS. combines with Charles Brown's transcript (3.11) to complete the text of this fragmentary work.

**3.11**
Brown transcript; I.i.1 to I.ii.19a only. KeJ 207.

**fMS Eng 1274**   Brown transcript. KeJ 209.

### In drear nighted December
("Stanzas") G.551; A.287; S.221.

**3.1, f.19$^v$**   Woodhouse transcript. KeJ 179.

**3.2, f.15$^r$**   Woodhouse transcript. KeJ 178.

**3.12, f.70$^v$**   Towers transcript.

**3.13, I, f.25$^v$**   W. P. Woodhouse transcript.

### In midmost Ind, beside Hydaspes cool
("The Jealousies"; "The Cap and Bells") G.395; A.701; S.504.

**2.29.1**      A.MS., fragment of draft with revisions, lines 109-144. 2p. on 1 leaf, 20.1 x 12.3 cm. Wove paper watermarked: C Wil[mott] | 18[  ]. KeJ 204. Stillinger, pp. 246-249.

In Dodd, Mead & Co. catalogue, January 1899, p.38; A. S. W. Rosenbach. Bequeathed by Amy Lowell, 1925.

**2.29.2**   A.MS., fragment of draft with revisions, lines 397-459; on the last verso, the unassociated fragment beginning: *This living hand, now warm and capable.* 4p. on 2 conjunct leaves, 20 x 24.7 cm. Wove paper unwatermarked. KeJ 204. Stillinger, pp.250-257.

William Harris Arnold (sale, Anderson, 10-11 November 1924, lot 505). Bequeathed by Amy Lowell, 1925.

**3.2, f.196ʳ**   Woodhouse transcript. KeJ 205.

**fMS Eng 1274**   Brown transcript. KeJ 206.

---

*In short, convince you that however wise*
("Fragment of Castle-builder")
G.500; A.390; S.286.

**3.2, f.134ʳ**   Woodhouse transcript. KeJ 106.

---

*In thy western halls of gold*
("Ode to Apollo") G.429; A.14; S.34.

**3.2, f.221ʳ**   Woodhouse transcript. KeJ 288.

**4.20.9**   Woodhouse transcript. KeJ 289.

---

*It keeps eternal whisperings around*
("On the Sea") G.460; A.112; S.95.

**3.1, f.18ᵛ**   Woodhouse transcript. KeJ 353.

**3.2, f.26ʳ**   Woodhouse transcript. KeJ 352.

**3.3, p.44**   Woodhouse transcript. KeJ 349.

**3.10(14)**   Patmore transcript. KeJ 357.

**3.10(23)**   Patmore transcript. KeJ 358.

**4.20.9**   Woodhouse transcript. KeJ 355.

**4.20.10**   Woodhouse transcript. KeJ 356.

---

*Keen, fitful gusts are whisp'ring here and there*
G.44; A.63; S.64.

**3.12, f.47ʳ**   Stephens transcript.

---

*Light feet, dark violet eyes, and parted hair*
(stanza 2 of *Woman! when I behold thee. . .*)
G.26; A.43; S.40.

**3.12, f.27ᵛ**   Stephens transcript.

---

*Lo! I must tell a tale of chivalry*
("Specimen of an Induction to a Poem")
G.12; A.33; S.47.

**3.5, p.1**   Tom Keats transcript. KeJ 405.

**3.12, f.11ʳ**   Stephens transcript.

---

*Many the wonders I this day have seen*
("To My Brother George") G.39; A.47; S.55.

**2.2**   A.MS. in pencil; first draft, with cancelled lines and numerous revisions on pp. 6-7 of the so-called "Severn pocket-book," which consists of 8p. on 4 leaves, 11.7 x 6.7 cm.; also containing the octave of *Small, busy flames play through the fresh laid coals*, two drafts of a letter from Tom Keats to Richard Abbey, and a drawing and some miscellaneous notes by an unidentified hand. Wove paper watermarked: [ ]ARKI[ ] | 1813. KeJ 502. Stillinger, pp. 8-9.

Joseph Severn; Dr. Valeriani (inheritor of Severn's Keats MSS in 1879); Henry Sotheran; F. Holland Day; Frank J. Hogan (sale, Parke-Bernet, 25 April 1945, lot 431) to A. S. W. Rosenbach; Dr. C. Ernest Cooke (sale, Parke-Bernet, 4 June 1969, lot 93). Presented by Arthur A. Houghton, Jr., 1969.

Garrod wrongly ascribes this MS. to the Huntington Library, which never owned it; Allott repeats the error.

For a fuller discussion of this MS., see Robert Gittings, "A Draft of the Earliest Known Letter of Keats's Brother Tom," *Harvard Library Bulletin*, 19:3 (July 1971) 285-289.

**2.3**   A.MS., fair copy with a few corrections, probably that sent to the press (see 2.7). 1p. on 1 leaf, 17.2 x 12.2 cm. Laid paper, unidentifiable fragment of watermark. KeJ 503. Stillinger, pp. 10-11.

Endorsed in unidentified hand on verso: "Autograph Sonnet by Keats Received from M.ʳ Waller April 1846." The leaf was evidently once pasted in an album, and is numbered in the upper right corner "53." Leonard G. Stowell (sale, Sotheby, 20 December 1937, lot 260). Presented by Arthur A. Houghton, Jr., 1970.

**3.4, f.34ᵛ**   George Keats transcript. KeJ 504.

**3.5, p.14**   Tom Keats transcript. KeJ 505.

**3.12, f.43ʳ**   Stephens transcript.

---

### *Minutes are flying swiftly; and as yet*
("On Receiving a Laurel Crown from Leigh Hunt") G.529; A.109; S.90.

**Keats \*EC8.K2262.817p (G), p.78**
A.MS., fair copy. Written in the copy of *Poems* (1817) presented to John Hamilton Reynolds. KeJ 332. Stillinger, pp. 46-47. This MS. is the sole source for the two laurel crown sonnets.

For provenance, see *Forgive me, Haydon, that I cannot speak*.

---

### *Mother of Hermes! and still youthful Maia!*
("Ode to May") G.488; A.353; S.264.

**3.2, f.132ʳ**   Woodhouse transcript. KeJ 243.

**3.3, p.65**   In Woodhouse transcript of letter to John Hamilton Reynolds, 3 May 1818. KeJ 242. Rollins 80.

**4.20.9**   Woodhouse transcript. KeJ 244.

---

### *Much have I travell'd in the realms of gold*
("On First Looking into Chapman's Homer") G.45; A.60; S.64.

**2.4**   A.MS., early draft, differing from published version. 1p. on 1 leaf, 19.8 x 15.8 cm. Laid paper, fragment of crown watermark. On verso, in unidentified hand, headed "Burns Letters," is the first paragraph of the letter from Robert Burns to Helen Maria Williams, 1789; see *The Letters of Robert Burns*, ed. J. DeLancey Ferguson (Oxford, 1931) I, 352, no. 358. KeJ 321. Stillinger, pp. 12-13.

Same provenance as 1.5.

**3.5, p.18**   Tom Keats transcript. KeJ 323.

**3.12, f.48ʳ**   Stephens transcript.

---

### *My heart aches, and a drowsy numbness pains*
("Ode to a Nightingale") G.257; A.523; S.369.

**3.1, f.82ʳ**   Woodhouse transcript. KeJ 286.

**3.2, f.157ʳ**   Woodhouse transcript. KeJ 283.

---

### *My spirit is too weak—mortality*
("On Seeing the Elgin Marbles") G.478; A.104; S.93.

**Keats \*EC8.K2262.817p (G), p.122**
A.MS., written in the copy of *Poems* (1817) presented to John Hamilton Reynolds. KeJ 333. Stillinger, pp. 48-49.

For provenance, see *Forgive me, Haydon, that I cannot speak*.

**3.2, f.21ʳ**   Woodhouse transcript. KeJ 335.

**4.7.20**   Haydon transcript.

**4.20.10**   Woodhouse transcript. KeJ 337.

*Nature withheld Cassandra in the skies*
("Translated from Ronsard")
G.497; A.383; S.285.

**3.2, f.140ʳ**    Woodhouse transcript. KeJ 248.


*No, no, go not to Lethe, neither twist*
("Ode on Melancholy") G.274; A.538; S.374.

**3.2, f.145ʳ**    Woodhouse transcript. KeJ 281.

**3.6, p.7**    Brown transcript. KeJ 279.

See also: *Though you should build a bark of dead men's bones.*


*No! those days are gone away*
("Robin Hood") G.166; A.301; S.228.

**3.1, f.8ᵛ**    Woodhouse transcript. KeJ 386.

**3.2, f.58ʳ**    Woodhouse transcript. KeJ 383.

**3.6, p.1**    Brown transcript. KeJ 384.


*Not Aladdin magian*
("On Visiting Staffa") G.493; A.372; S.277.

**1.35**    A.MS. in letter to Tom Keats, 23–26 July 1818. KeJ 250. Rollins 100.

**3.1, f.69ʳ**    Woodhouse transcript. KeJ 254.

**3.2, f.62ʳ**    Woodhouse transcript. KeJ 252.


*Now Morning from her orient chamber came*
("Imitation of Spenser") G.25; A.3; S.27.

**3.5, p.12**    Tom Keats transcript. KeJ 174.

**3.12, f.25ᵛ**    Stephens transcript.


*Nymph of the downward smile, and sidelong glance*
("To G[eorgiana] A[ugusta] W[ylie]")
G.42; A.98; S.67.

**3.4, f.31ᵛ**    A.MS., fair copy, pasted on page of Georgiana Keats's scrapbook. 1p. on 1 leaf, 13.5 x 11.8 cm. Wove paper unwatermarked; different from the paper of the scrapbook. KeJ 475. Stillinger, pp. 22-23.

**3.5, p.21**    Tom Keats transcript. KeJ 476.

**3.12, f.45ᵛ**    Stephens transcript.

**3.13,II, f.3ᵛ**    W. P. Woodhouse transcript. KeJ 477.


*O blush not so! O blush not so!*
("Song") G.544; A.298; S.226.

**3.3, p.53**    In Woodhouse transcript of letter to John Hamilton Reynolds, 31 January 1818. KeJ 257. Rollins 58.

**3.6, p.6**    Brown transcript. KeJ 256.


*O come, dearest Emma! the rose is full blown*
("To Emma") G.542; A.21; S.39.

**3.2, f.219ʳ**    Woodhouse transcript. KeJ 262.

**3.4, f.35ʳ**    George Keats transcript, beginning *O come Georgiana.* KeJ 263.

**4.20.9**    Woodhouse transcript. KeJ 264.


*O Goddess! hear these tuneless numbers, wrung*
("Ode to Psyche") G.262; A.514; S.364.

**1.53**    A.MS. in letter to George and Georgiana Keats, 14 February–3 May 1819. KeJ 291. Rollins 159.

**3.2, f.72ʳ**    Woodhouse transcript. KeJ 293.

**3.6, p.36**    Brown transcript. KeJ 292.

***O golden-tongued Romance, with serene lute!***
("On Sitting Down to Read *King Lear* Once
Again") G.483; A.295; S.225.

**3.1, f.16ᵛ**     Woodhouse transcript. KeJ 345.

**3.2, f.25ʳ**     Woodhouse transcript. KeJ 342.

**3.6, p.50**     Brown transcript. KeJ 343.

**3.9, f.4ʳ**     Jeffrey transcript. KeJ 341.

***O grant that like to Peter I***
G.568; A.753; S.100.

**2.31**     A.MS., two versions. 1p. on 1 leaf,
the detached back cover of a marbled paper
notebook, 22 x 18.2 cm. Wove paper
unwatermarked. KeJ 265. Stillinger, pp. 56-57.
This MS. is the sole source for these lines.

Same provenance as 1.14. Presented by Arthur A.
Houghton, Jr., 1970.

***O soft embalmer of the still midnight***
("Sonnet to Sleep") G.467; A.510; S.363.

**1.53**     A.MS. in letter to George and
Georgiana Keats, 14 February–3 May 1819.
KeJ 399. Rollins 159.

**3.1, f.79ʳ**     Woodhouse transcript. KeJ 404.

**3.2, f.151ʳ**     Woodhouse transcript. KeJ 401.

**3.6, p.48**     Brown transcript. KeJ 402.

***O Solitude! if I must with thee dwell***
G.42; A.22; S.41.

**3.5, p.23**     Tom Keats transcript. KeJ 268.

**3.12, f.46ʳ**     Stephens transcript.

***O that a week could be an age, and we***
("To J[ames] R[ice]") G.465; A.351; S.244.

**2.18**     A.MS., draft with revisions. 1p. on
1 leaf, 24.5 x 19.7 cm. Laid paper watermarked
with fleur-de-lys. KeJ 489. Stillinger, pp. 68-69.

Same provenance as 1.6 (lot 558 in sale, 1903). The col-
lection also includes the copy of Matteo Aleman,
*Guzman de Alfarache* (1634) said to have inspired this
sonnet (Keats *EC8.K2262.Zz634a).

**3.2, f.218ʳ**     Woodhouse transcript. KeJ 490.

**3.10(10)**     Patmore transcript. KeJ 492.

**4.20.9**     Woodhouse transcript. KeJ 491.

***O thou whose face hath felt the winter's wind***
G.482; A.310; S.235.

**3.3, p.25**     In Woodhouse transcript of letter to
John Hamilton Reynolds, 19 February 1818.
KeJ 270. Rollins 62.

***O were I one of the Olympian twelve***
("Extracts from an Opera") G.438; A.313; S.235.

**3.2, f.137ʳ**     Woodhouse transcript. KeJ 84.

**3.6, p.42**     Brown transcript. KeJ 83.

***O what can ail thee, knight at arms***
("La Belle Dame sans Merci: A Ballad")
G.441; A.500; S.357.

**1.53**     A.MS. in letter to George and
Georgiana Keats, 14 February–3 May 1819.
KeJ 210. Rollins 159.

**3.1, f.73ʳ**     Woodhouse transcript. KeJ 213.

**3.2, f.76ʳ**     Woodhouse transcript. KeJ 212.

**3.6, p.9**     Brown transcript. KeJ 211.

*Of late two dainties were before me plac'd*
G.537; A.369; S.274.

**3.10(26)**     Unidentified transcript. KeJ 295.


*Oft have you seen a swan superbly frowning*
("To Charles Cowden Clarke") G.35; A.54; S.60.

**3.12, f.37ᵛ**     Stephens transcript.


*Oh Chatterton! how very sad thy fate*
("To Chatterton") G.476; A.10; S.32.

**3.2, f.216ʳ**     Woodhouse transcript. KeJ 297.

**4.20.9**     Woodhouse transcript. KeJ 298.


*Oh! how I love, on a fair summer's eve*
G.457; A.46; S.54.

**3.1, f.13ʳ**     Woodhouse transcript. KeJ 301.

**3.2, f.9ʳ**     Woodhouse transcript. KeJ 299.

**3.10(7)**     Patmore transcript. KeJ 304.

**4.20.9**     Woodhouse transcript. KeJ 303.


*Oh Peace! and dost thou with thy presence bless*
("On Peace") G.527; A.5; S.28.

**3.2, f.220ʳ**     Woodhouse transcript. KeJ 326.

**4.20.9**     Woodhouse transcript. KeJ 327.


*Old Meg she was a gipsey*
G.490; A.358; S.266.

**1.33**     A.MS. in letter to Tom Keats,
3–9 July 1818. KeJ 306. Rollins 95.


*One morn before me were three figures seen*
("Ode on Indolence") G.447; A.541; S.375.

**3.2, f.147ʳ**     Woodhouse transcript. KeJ 276.

**3.6, p.19**     Brown transcript. KeJ 275.


*Over the hill and over the dale*
G.487; A.319; S.240.

**1.25**     A.MS. in letter to James Rice,
24 March 1818. KeJ 377. Rollins 72.

**3.3, p.113**     Woodhouse transcript. KeJ 379.


*Physician Nature! let my spirit blood!*
("To Fanny") G.454; A.739; S.494.

**2.30**     A.MS., fragment of draft with
revisions, lines 9-24, 33-56. 3p. on 3 leaves, 24.7 x
20 cm. (the second now lacking its top half, 15.6
x 20 cm.). Wove paper watermarked: [C]
Wɪʟᴍᴏᴛᴛ | 1818. KeJ 473. Stillinger, pp. 226-231.

Same provenance as 1.14.

**3.10(6)**     Milnes transcript. KeJ 474.


*Pleasures lie thickest where no pleasures seem*
A forgery; see 6.1.


*Read me a lesson, Muse, and speak it loud*
G.495; A.375; S.279.

**1.36**     A.MS. in letter to Tom Keats,
3 August 1818. KeJ 381. Rollins 101.


*St. Agnes' Eve—Ah, bitter chill it was*
("The Eve of St. Agnes") G.236; A.450; S.299.

**2.21**     A.MS., early draft, heavily revised,
of lines 64-378 (end); lines 1-63, not known to
survive in autograph, supplied in the hand of

Frederick Locker. 19p. on 5 leaves, written 2p. to the side, each leaf with an irregular stub at the left edge; 20.2 x 29.7 cm. to 20.2 x 26.4 cm. Wove paper unwatermarked; heavily treated and silked for preservation, probably because of the accident related by S. Foster Damon in *Amy Lowell* (Boston, 1935), p. 528. KeJ 72. Stillinger, pp. 94-131.

MS. affidavit of authenticity signed by Joseph Severn and inscribed: "Signed Sealed and declared by M.ʳ Joseph Severn at Rome the 27ᵗʰ day of May 1879 before me Alex[ander] Roesler Franz British Viceconsul Rome," with vice-consular stamp and wax seal; after that, same provenance as 1.5.

**1.80**      A.MS. revisions of certain lines, in letter to John Taylor, 11 June 1820. KeJ 76. Rollins 263.

**3.1, f.54ʳ**      Woodhouse transcript. KeJ 75.

**3.2, f.110ʳ**      Woodhouse transcript. KeJ 73.

### Season of mists and mellow fruitfulness
("To Autumn") G.273; A.650; S.476.

**1.64**      A.MS. in letter to Richard Woodhouse, 21 September 1819. KeJ 468. Rollins 194.

**2.27**      A.MS., early draft, with revisions. 2p. on 1 leaf, 24.7 x 19.9 cm. Wove paper watermarked: C WILMOTT | 1818. KeJ 467. Stillinger, pp. 222-225.

George Keats; Anna H. Barker (later Mrs. Anna H. B. Ward); Elizabeth Ward (later Mrs. Elizabeth W. Perkins), who presented it to Amy Lowell in 1921. Bequeathed, 1925.

**3.2, f.142ʳ**      Woodhouse transcript. KeJ 471.

**3.6, p.34**      Brown transcript.

### Shed no tear—O shed no tear!
("Fairy's Song") G.436; A.489; S.377.

**2.22**      A.MS., fair copy. 1p. on 1 leaf, 20 x 12.5 cm. Laid paper, fragment of unidentified watermark. Inscribed on verso by Charles Brown: "A faery Song written for a particular purpose at the request of C[harles] B[rown]." KeJ 390. Stillinger, pp. 140-141.

Same provenance as 1.14.

**3.10(4)**      Milnes transcript. KeJ 392.

### Small, busy flames play through the fresh laid coals
("To My Brothers") G.43; A.65; S.66.

**2.2**      A.MS. in pencil, octave only. On p.8 of the "Severn pocket-book"; for description, see under *Many the wonders I this day have seen*. KeJ 506. Stillinger, pp. 14-15.

**2.5**      A.MS., fair copy, but with two revisions; headed in the hand of Charles Ollier, "1817 This was copy for the press." On verso, A.MS. of lines 231-235 of *I stood tip-toe upon a little hill*. 2p. on 1 leaf, 11.8 x 10.3 cm. Wove paper unwatermarked. KeJ 508. Stillinger, pp. 18-19. Stillinger disputes Ollier's statement.

Charles Ollier; sale, Puttick and Simpson, 19 July 1877, lot 98; Alfred Morrison (sale, Sotheby, 13 December 1917, lot 575); W. T. Spencer. Presented by Arthur A. Houghton, Jr., 1970.

**2.6**      A.MS., fair copy. 1p. on 1 leaf, 19.8 x 15.2 cm. Laid paper, fragment of crown watermark. Dated by Keats "Novʳ. 28." KeJ 507. Stillinger, pp. 16-17.

Once pasted in Emma Isola Moxon's autograph album; appeared in Quaritch catalogues (August 1884, no. 21887; September 1886, no. 35885); John A. Spoor (sale, Parke-Bernet, 28 April 1939, lot 520). Presented by Arthur A. Houghton, Jr., 1970.

**3.5, p.16**      Tom Keats transcript. KeJ 509.

**3.12, f.46ᵛ**      Stephens transcript.

***So, I am safe emerged from these broils***
("Otho the Great") G.311; A.544; S.378.

**2.24.1**     A.MS., fragment of draft, with revisions, comprising I.i.17-24. 1p. on 1 leaf, slip cut from a larger sheet; 11.7 x 20.1 cm. Laid paper watermarked: [C WIL]MOTT | [18]18. KeJ 370. Stillinger, pp. 142-143.

Joseph Severn; John W. Field. Presented by Arthur A. Houghton, Jr., 1970.

**2.24.2**     A.MS., fragment of draft, with revisions, comprising I.i.34-44a. 1p. on 1 leaf, slip cut from a larger sheet; 10.6 x 20 cm. Thick wove paper unwatermarked. KeJ 370. Stillinger, pp. 142-143.

Joseph Severn; Frederick Locker (not recorded in *The Rowfant Catalogue* or its *Supplement*); in Edwin H. Denham catalogue XIII, 1902, no. 92; Dodd, Mead & Co. catalogue 95, November 1909, no. 200. Bequeathed by Amy Lowell, 1925.

**2.24.3**     A.MS., fragment of original draft, with revisions, comprising IV.i.76-85. 1p. on 1 leaf, slip cut from a larger sheet; 12 x 18.4 cm. Laid paper watermarked: Gilling | & | Allford | 1816. KeJ 366. Stillinger, pp. 144-145.

George Keats; Emma Keats Speed; M. A. D. Hunt; Mattie Franklin Chenault; Mrs. Ephraim Whitman Gurney. Presented by Mrs. John Briggs Potter, 1955.

**2.24.4**     A.MS., fragment of original draft, with revisions, comprising IV.ii.121b-126. 1p. on 1 leaf, irregularly shaped slip cut from a larger sheet, evidently originally 11.7 x 21.2 cm.; piece cut away from top, reducing principal dimensions to 6.9 x 21.2 cm. Laid paper unwatermarked. This fragment and the next were originally part of the same sheet. KeJ 367. Stillinger, pp. 144-145.

Joseph Severn; Miss [Geraldine Endsor?] Jewsbury; Thomas Bailey Aldrich. Presented by Talbot Aldrich, 1943.

**2.24.5**     A.MS., fragment of original draft, with revisions, comprising IV.ii.127-139 (recto), V.i.18-32(verso). 2p. on 1 leaf, 27 x 22 cm. Laid paper watermarked: I S | 1810. KeJ 367. Stillinger, pp. 146-149.

Joseph Severn; James T. Fields. Presented by Mrs. James T. Fields, 1915.

**2.24.6**     A.MS., fragment of original draft, with revisions, comprising V.ii.8b-15. 1p. on 1 leaf, slip cut from a larger sheet; 9.8 x 22.2 cm. Laid paper unwatermarked. KeJ 367. Stillinger, pp. 150-151.

Joseph Severn; Mrs. Bruen. Presented by George Benson Weston, 1946.

**2.24.7**     A.MS., fragment of original draft, with revisions, comprising V.v.151b-164a(recto), 173c-174(verso). 2p. on 1 leaf, slip cut from a larger sheet; 16.8 x 21.4 cm. Laid paper watermarked with fleur-de-lys. KeJ 367. Stillinger, pp. 150-153.

Joseph Severn; Miss C. M. Beresford; in Dodd, Mead & Co. catalogue 106, November 1903; Archer M. Huntington; American Academy of Arts and Letters (sale, Sotheby, 12 November 1963, lot 88). Presented by Arthur A. Houghton, Jr., 1963.

**3.7**     Charles Brown transcript of complete text, except I.i.1-18, IV.ii.3-45, V.i.30-ii.27; with autograph revisions by John Keats. KeJ 374.

**fMS Eng 1274**     Brown transcript. KeJ 376.

***Son of the old moon-mountains African!***
("To the Nile") G.484; A.307; S.233.

**3.1, f.18^r**     Woodhouse transcript. KeJ 518.

**3.2, f.27^r**     Woodhouse transcript. KeJ 517.

**3.6, p.54**     Brown transcript; lines 6-8 in the hand of John Keats. KeJ 516.

### Souls of poets dead and gone
("Lines on the Mermaid Tavern")
G.269; A.304; S.230.

**2.16**    A.MS., fair copy. 1p. on 1 leaf, 25.3 x 20.2 cm.; a piece approximately 2.6 x 9.7 cm. torn from the top left corner. Laid paper watermarked: 1814. KeJ 234. Stillinger, pp. 66-67.

Same provenance as 1.14.

**3.1, f.10$^v$**    Woodhouse transcript. KeJ 239.

**3.1, f.77$^r$**    Woodhouse transcript. KeJ 239.

**3.2, f.61$^r$**    Woodhouse transcript. KeJ 237.

**3.6, p.4**    Brown transcript. KeJ 236.

### Spenser, a jealous honorer of thine
G.476; A.308; S.233.

**3.2, f.144$^r$**    Woodhouse transcript. KeJ 410.

**3.10(18)**    Longmore transcript. KeJ 412.

**4.20.9**    Woodhouse transcript. KeJ 411.

### Spirit here that reignest!
("Song") G.436; A.388; S.295.

**3.6, p.59**    Brown transcript. KeJ 414.

### Standing aloof in giant ignorance
("To Homer") G.463; A.352; S.264.

**3.1, f.73$^r$**    Woodhouse transcript. KeJ 486.

**3.2, f.78$^r$**    Woodhouse transcript. KeJ 485.

**3.6, p.40**    Brown transcript, with five words in the hand of John Keats. KeJ 484.

### Stay, ruby breasted warbler, stay
("Song") G.543; A.744; S.29.

**3.2, f.219$^r$**    Woodhouse transcript. KeJ 418.

**3.4, f.6$^v$**    Georgiana Keats transcript. KeJ 415.

**3.4, f.32$^r$**    George Keats transcript. KeJ 419.

**3.10(15)**    Patmore transcript. KeJ 421.

**4.20.9**    Woodhouse transcript. KeJ 420.

### Sweet are the pleasures that to verse belong
("To George Felton Mathew") G.28; A.24; S.41.

**3.12, f.30$^r$**    Stephens transcript.

### Sweet, sweet is the greeting of eyes
G.547; A.356; S.265.

**1.32**    A.MS. in letter to George and Georgiana Keats, 27–28 June 1818. KeJ 422. Rollins 92.

### The church bells toll a melancholy round
("Written in Disgust of Vulgar Superstition") G.532; A.97; S.88.

**2.10**    A.MS., first draft. 1p. on 1 leaf, 18.5 x 12 cm. Wove paper unwatermarked. Written on the verso of A.L. (signature cut away) from George Keats to John and Tom Keats, [August 1816], Rollins 4. "J Keats" and "Written in 15 minutes" added by Tom Keats. KeJ 550. Stillinger, pp. 44-45.

Formerly tipped in a copy of *Endymion* (1818); Thomas Jefferson McKee (sale, Anderson, 17 February 1902, lot 4004); John A. Spoor (sale, Parke-Bernet, 27 April 1939, lot 463). Presented by Arthur A. Houghton, Jr., 1946.

**3.5, p.19**    Tom Keats transcript. KeJ 551.

**3.10(1)**    Unidentified transcript. KeJ 553.

**3.12, f.69$^r$**    Stephens transcript. KeJ 552.

*The day is gone, and all its sweets are gone!*
G.473; A.685; S.491.

**3.2, f.212ʳ**     Woodhouse transcript. KeJ 425.

**3.6, p.57**     Brown transcript. KeJ 424.

**4.20.9**     Woodhouse transcript. KeJ 427.

*The Gothic looks solemn*
("Lines Rhymed in a Letter from Oxford")
G.554; A.284; S.99.

**3.1, f.19ʳ**     Woodhouse transcript. KeJ 429.

**3.2, f.29ʳ**     Woodhouse transcript. KeJ 428.

*The poetry of earth is never dead*
("On the Grasshopper and Cricket")
G.49; A.97; S.88.

**3.12, f.50ʳ**     Stephens transcript.

*The town, the churchyard, and the setting sun*
("On Visiting the Tomb of Burns")
G.489; A.357; S.266.

**3.9, f.7ʳ**     Jeffrey transcript. KeJ 362.

*There is a joy in footing slow across a silent plain*
("Lines Written in the Highlands After a Visit to Burns's Country") G.491; A.370; S.275.

**1.34**     A.MS. in letter to Benjamin Bailey, 18–22 July 1818. KeJ 432. Rollins 99.

**2.19**     A.MS., draft with revisions. 2p. on 1 leaf, 32.6 x 27.5 cm. Laid paper watermarked with Britannia seated in a crowned oval. KeJ 431. Stillinger, pp. 88-91.

Same provenance as 1.14.

**3.2, f.213ʳ**     Woodhouse transcript. KeJ 434.

*Think not of it, sweet one, so*
G.432; A.285; S.100.

**3.1, f.12ᵛ**     Woodhouse transcript. KeJ 441.

**3.2, f.16ʳ**     Woodhouse transcript. KeJ 440.

**4.4.4**     Clarke transcript. KeJ 443.

*This living hand, now warm and capable*
G.553; A.700; S.503.

**2.29.2**     A.MS., draft, written on last verso of MS. fragment of "The Jealousies"; for details, see *In midmost Ind, beside Hydaspes cool.* KeJ 444. Stillinger, pp. 258-259. This MS. is the sole source for these lines.

*This pleasant tale is like a little copse*
("Written on a Blank Space at the End of Chaucer's Tale 'The floure and the lefe'")
G.459; A.103; S.92.

**3.1, f.14ᵛ**     Woodhouse transcript. KeJ 448.

**3.2, f.19ᵛ**     Woodhouse transcript. KeJ 446.

**3.10(13)**     Patmore transcript. KeJ 450.

**3.12, f.70ʳ**     Towers transcript. KeJ 447.

**4.20.9**     Woodhouse transcript. KeJ 449.

*Thou still unravish'd bride of quietness*
("Ode on a Grecian Urn") G.260; A.532; S.372.

**3.2, f.188ʳ**     Woodhouse transcript. KeJ 273.

**3.6, p.25**     Brown transcript. KeJ 271.

*Though you should build a bark of dead men's bones*
("Ode on Melancholy"; cancelled first stanza)
G.503; A.538; S.374.

**3.2, f.145ʳ**     Woodhouse transcript.

**3.6, p.7**     Brown transcript.

*Time's sea hath been five years at its slow ebb*
("To———") G.466; A.306; S.232.

**3.1, f.17ʳ**    Woodhouse transcript. KeJ 453.

**3.2, f.28ʳ**    Woodhouse transcript. KeJ 451.

**3.10(11)**    Patmore transcript. KeJ 455.

**4.20.9**    Woodhouse transcript. KeJ 454.

**4.20.10**    Woodhouse transcript. KeJ 456.

*'Tis the "witching time of night"*
G.495; A.384; S.288.

**1.39**    A.MS. in letter to George and
Georgiana Keats, 14–31 October 1818.
KeJ 457. Rollins 120.

**3.10(19)**    Payne transcript. KeJ 458.

*To one who has been long in city pent*
G.44; A.45; S.53.

**3.4, f.5ʳ**    Georgiana Keats transcript. KeJ 510.

**3.4, f.32ᵛ**    George Keats transcript. KeJ 511.

**3.5, p.24**    Tom Keats transcript. KeJ 512.

**3.12, f.47ᵛ**    Stephens transcript.

*Two or three posies*
G.566; A.522; S.368.

**1.52**    A.MS. in letter to Fanny Keats,
1 May 1819. KeJ 522. Rollins 158.

*Unfelt, unheard, unseen*
G.433; A.44; S.96.

**4.4.4**    Clarke transcript. KeJ 526.

*Upon a Sabbath day it fell*
("The Eve of St. Mark") G.449; A.480; S.319.

**3.2, f.125ʳ**    Woodhouse transcript. KeJ 82.

**3.6, p.29**    Brown transcript. KeJ 80.

*Upon a time, before the faery broods*
("Lamia") G.191; A.613; S.452.

**1.63**    A.MS. of II.122-162 and 15 cancelled
lines, in letter to John Taylor, 5 September 1819.
KeJ 222. Rollins 90.

**2.25**    A.MS., fragment of early draft,
heavily revised; comprising II.26-49, 85-92
(preceded and followed by ten lines
subsequently discarded and two others that
were used in II.104-105), 122-147, 191-198. 4p. on
2 leaves, 32.5 x 20 cm. Laid paper watermarked:
BEECH MILL | 1818, with countermark of
seated Britannia in a crowned oval. KeJ 218
and KeJ 221. Stillinger, pp. 154-161.

Same provenance as 1.14.

**2.26**    A.MS., fair copy but with numerous
revisions and cancellations, evidently the
printers' manuscript. 30p. on 26 leaves, 33 x 16.7
cm. Laid paper watermarked: BEECH MILL |
1818, with countermark of Britannia in a
crowned oval. Bound in modern green
morocco by Rivière. On verso of last leaf, in
pencil rubbed and nearly illegible, notes and/
or layouts in a hand similar to that appearing in
Woodhouse commonplace book 3.1,
concerning contents and price of *Lamia* (1820)
KeJ 223. Stillinger, pp. 162-221.

Family of John Taylor (sale, Sotheby, 10 March 1897,
lot 720) to J. Pearson, bookseller; William A. White;
Frank B. Bemis; sold privately by A. S. W. Rosenbach.
Presented by Arthur A. Houghton, Jr., 1970.

**Keats *EC8.K2262.8201a**
Page proofs for the first edition (1820),
corrected and annotated by JK, Richard
Woodhouse, and John Taylor. 52 leaves
(pp. [1]-45, interleaved with blanks); 17.2 cm.
Sewn, unbound. KeJ 224.

Richard Woodhouse; Frank B. Bemis; Arthur A.
Houghton, Jr. Presented, 1950.

*Upon my life, Sir Nevis, I am piqu'd*
G.561; A.376; S.279.

**1.36**        A.MS. in letter to Tom Keats,
3 August 1818. KeJ 527. Rollins 101.

*Welcome joy, and welcome sorrow*
G.502; A.386; S.231.

**3.1, f.75ʳ**     Woodhouse transcript. KeJ 531.

**3.2, f.133ʳ**    Woodhouse transcript. KeJ 529.

**3.6, p.52**      Brown transcript. KeJ 528.

**3.12, f.67ᵛ**    Stephens transcript. KeJ 533.

**4.4.4**          Clarke transcript. KeJ 534.

*What is more gentle than a wind in summer?*
("Sleep and Poetry") G.51; A.69; S.69.

**3.12, f.53ʳ**    Stephens transcript.

*What is there in the universal earth*
("To the Ladies Who Saw Me Crown'd")
G.530; A.110; S.90.

**Keats *EC8.K2262.817p (G), p.78**
A.MS., fair copy, written in the copy of *Poems*
(1817) presented to John Hamilton Reynolds.
KeJ 515. Stillinger, pp. 46-47.

For provenance, see *Forgive me, Haydon, that I cannot
speak.*

*What sylph-like form before my eyes*
A forgery; see 6.2.

*What though, for showing truth to flatter'd state*
("Written on the Day That Mr. Leigh Hunt
Left Prison") G.40; A.11; S.32.

**3.12, f.44ʳ**    Stephens transcript. KeJ 556.

*What though while the wonders of nature
exploring*
("To Some Ladies") G.18; A.18; S.36.

**3.12, f.18ʳ**    Stephens transcript.

*When by my solitary hearth I sit*
("To Hope") G.23; A.12; S.33.

**3.12, f.23ᵛ**    Stephens transcript.

*When I have fears that I may cease to be*
G.462; A.296; S.225.

**3.1, f.72ʳ**     Woodhouse transcript. KeJ 539.

**3.2, f.64ʳ**     Woodhouse transcript. KeJ 538.

**3.3, p.55**      In Woodhouse transcript of letter to
John Hamilton Reynolds, 31 January 1818.
KeJ 537. Rollins 58.

**3.6, p.39**      Brown transcript. KeJ 535.

**4.20.10**        Woodhouse transcript. KeJ 541.

*When they were come unto the Faery's court*
G.563; A.491; S.323.

**1.53**           A.MS. in letter to George and
Georgiana Keats, 14 February–3 May 1819.
KeJ 542. Rollins 159.

*Where be ye going, you Devon maid*
G.546; A.318; S.240.

**1.24**　　A.MS. in letter to Benjamin Robert Haydon, 21 March 1818. KeJ 543. Rollins 70.

**Keats *EC8.K2262.W848ma**
Transcript by unknown hand in v.1 of Richard Monckton Milnes, *Life, Letters and Literary Remains of John Keats* (London, 1848). Same hand as 3.10.27 to 30.

*Where's the Poet? Show him! show him!*
("Fragment") G.499; A.389; S.290.

**3.2, f.187ʳ**　　Woodhouse transcript. KeJ 546.

**3.6, p.35**　　Brown transcript. KeJ 544.

*Which of the fairest three*
("Apollo to the Graces") G.545; A.290; S.222.

**2.14**
A.MS., draft, with revisions. 1p. on 1 leaf, 22.8 x 18.8 cm. Laid paper watermarked: GATER | 1816. KeJ 20. Stillinger, pp. 58-59.

Oliver R. Barrett (sale, Parke-Bernet, 30 October 1950, lot 638). Presented by Arthur A. Houghton, Jr., 1970.

**3.2, f.194ʳ**
Woodhouse transcript. KeJ 21.

*Who loves to peer up at the morning sun*
("On 'The Story of Rimini'") G.461; A.106; S.95.

**Keats *EC8.K2262.B829pa (B)**
Transcript by Leigh Hunt, on the last (blank) verso of his copy of *The Poetical Works of Coleridge, Shelley, and Keats* (1829). At bottom, also in Hunt's autograph, "Written by Keats in

a blank page of the 'presentation-copy' of his first volume of poems." (The "presentation-copy" is not now known to exist.) KeJ 359.

Leigh Hunt; Thornton Leigh Hunt; James T. Fields. Presented by Mrs. James T. Fields, 1915.

**3.6, p.24**　　Brown transcript. KeJ 361.

**4.9.3**　　Hunt transcript. KeJ 360.

*Why did I laugh tonight? No voice will tell*
G.470; A.488; S.323.

**1.53**　　A.MS. in letter to George and Georgiana Keats, 14 February–3 May 1819. KeJ 547. Rollins 159.

**3.9, f.25ʳ**　　Jeffrey transcript. KeJ 548.

**3.10(5)**　　Milnes transcript. KeJ 549.

*Woman! when I behold thee flippant, vain*
G.26; A.43; S.40.

**3.12, f.27ʳ**　　Stephens transcript.

**3.12, f.28ʳ**　　Stephens transcript (stanza 3).

**3.12, f.27ᵛ**　　Stephens transcript (stanza 2).

*You say you love; but with a voice*
("Stanzas") G.545; A.113; S.97.

**3.2, f.195ʳ**　　Woodhouse transcript.

*Young Calidore is paddling o'er the lake*
("Calidore") G.14; A.36; S.49.

**3.5, p.3**　　Tom Keats transcript. KeJ 55.

**3.12, f.13ʳ**　　Stephens transcript.

Let the winged Fancy roam,
Pleasure never is at home.

Steele

# Ode,
## On Indolence.
### 1819.

"They toil not, neither do they spin."

X

1

One morn before me were three figures seen,
With bowed necks, and joined hands, side-faced;
And one behind the other stepp'd serene,
In placid sandals, and in white robes graced:
They pass'd, like figures on a marble Urn,
When shifted round to see the other side;
They came again; as when the Urn once more
Is shifted round, the first seen Shades return;
And they were strange to me, as may betide
With Vases, to one deep in Phidian lore.

2

"Ode on Indolence." Transcript by Charles Armitage Brown (MS Keats 3.6, p.19).
Gift of Arthur A. Houghton, Jr., 1970.

# III. TRANSCRIPTS

*See also 4.20.6-.10.*

**3.1**

**Commonplace book of poems mainly by John Keats, compiled by Richard Woodhouse; summer of 1819.** All in Woodhouse's autograph, except "Hyperion" (22$^r$) by an amanuensis; with notes by H. Buxton Forman, Sir Sidney Colvin, and others (unidentified).

Brown diced calf notebook, rehinged; with printed front-matter, *The Literary Diary; or, Improved Common-place Book*, (London: Taylor & Hessey, 1811). 175 leaves ruled in blue, 24.2 x 19.4 cm. Laid paper watermarked: B B | 1809. In Garrod's and Stillinger's editions, assigned the siglum W$^1$.

Described in *The Woodhouse Poetry Transcripts at Harvard*, ed. by Jack Stillinger; volume 6 of *The Manuscripts of the Younger Romantics* (New York, 1988), pp. xv-xvi.

Richard Woodhouse; John Taylor; in the family until purchased by Sir Sidney Colvin in the 1880s; Robert Offley Ashburton Crewe-Milnes, Marquess of Crewe. Presented by Arthur A. Houghton, Jr., 1970.

## CONTENTS

*folio*

| | |
|---|---|
| 1$^r$ | Ownership inscriptions of George Taylor and Sir Sidney Colvin. |
| 2$^r$ | Letterpress title-page and introductory matter. |
| 6$^r$ | Trial layout in pencil of *Lamia* title-page. |
| 6$^v$ | Printed form for compiling index. |
| | After leaf 7, five stubs of excised leaves. |
| 8$^r$ | *God of the Meridian* (lines 13-25 only) |
| 8$^v$ | *No! those days are gone away* |
| 10$^r$ | Sonnets on Robin Hood by John Hamilton Reynolds. |
| 10$^v$ | *Souls of poets dead and gone* |
| 11$^r$ | Sonnet in a collection of MS. poetry, by John Hamilton Reynolds. |
| 11$^v$ | *Hadst thou lived in days of old* |
| 12$^v$ | *Think not of it, sweet one, so* |
| 13$^r$ | *Oh! how I love, on a fair summer's eve* |
| 13$^v$ | *As from the darkening gloom a silver dove* |
| 14$^r$ | *After dark vapours have oppress'd our plains* |
| 14$^v$ | *This pleasant tale is like a little copse* |
| 15$^r$ | Sonnet to Keats by John Hamilton Reynolds. |
| 15$^v$ | *Fresh morning gusts have blown away all fear* |
| 16$^r$ | *Cat! who has past thy grand climacteric* |
| 16$^v$ | *Oh golden tongued Romance with serene lute* |
| 17$^r$ | *Time's sea has been five years at its slow ebb* |
| 17$^v$ | *Blue! 'tis the life of Heaven—the domain* |
| 18$^r$ | *Son of the old Moon-Mountains African* |
| 18$^v$ | *It keeps eternal whisperings around* |
| 19$^r$ | *The Gothic looks solemn* |
| 19$^v$ | *In drear-nighted December* |
| 20$^v$ | *God of the golden bow* |
| 22$^r$ | *Deep in the shady sadness of a vale* (pencil notes by another hand on 27$^v$, 31$^v$, 33$^v$, 34$^v$, 35$^v$, 36$^v$, 37$^v$). Two of the original leaves apparently missing after leaf 53; they were presumably blank. |

54$^r$  *Saint Agnes' Eve—Ah bitter chill it was*
(pencil notes by another hand on 53$^v$, 57$^v$,
58$^v$, 59$^v$, 60$^v$, 65$^v$, 67$^v$)

69$^r$  *Not Aladdin magian*

71$^r$  *Bards of passion and of mirth*

72$^r$  *When I have fears that I may cease to be*

73$^r$  *Standing aloof in giant ignorance*

73$^v$  *O what can ail thee, knight at arms*

75$^r$  *Welcome joy and welcome sorrow*

77$^r$  *Souls of poets dead and gone*

78$^r$  *As Hermes once took to his feathers light*

79$^r$  *O soft embalmer of the still midnight*

79$^r$  *If by dull rhymes our English must be chain'd*

80$^r$  *Fame, like a wayward girl, will still be coy*

80$^r$  *Chief of organic numbers*

82$^r$  *My heart aches, and a drowsy numbness
pains*

86$^r$  *Fair Isabel, poor simple Isabel* (revisions and
notes in the hand of John Keats on 86$^v$, 91$^v$,
94$^r$, 98$^r$, 99$^r$, 101$^r$, 102$^r$; pencil or ink notes
by other hands *passim*)

108 to end      Blank, except for another trial
layout in pencil for the *Lamia* title-page,
on the last verso.

## 3.2

**Commonplace book of poems, etc., mainly
by John Keats, compiled by Richard
Woodhouse; dated November 1818;**
with some notes by other hands.

Notebook of marbled boards with brown calf
spine and corners. 233 leaves, 22.8 x 18.8 cm.
Laid paper watermarked: W ELGAR | 1805,
and a post-horn in an escutcheon. In Garrod's
and Stillinger's editions, assigned the siglum
W².

Published in facsimile in *The Woodhouse Poetry
Transcripts at Harvard*, ed. by Jack Stillinger;

volume 6 of *The Manuscripts of the Younger
Romantics* (New York, 1988).

Richard Woodhouse; John Taylor; in the Taylor
family until acquired by Robert Offley Ashburton
Crewe-Milnes, Marquess of Crewe. Presented by
Arthur A. Houghton, Jr., 1970.

## CONTENTS

*folio*

26<sup>r</sup>   *It keeps eternal whisperings around*

26<sup>v</sup>   Note on the next sonnet.

27<sup>r</sup>   *Son of the old Moon-Mountains African*

27<sup>v</sup>   Note on the next sonnet.

28<sup>r</sup>   *Time's sea hath been five years at its slow ebb*

29<sup>r</sup>   *The Gothic looks solemn*

29<sup>v</sup>   Note on the next poem.

30<sup>r</sup>   *Fair Isabel, poor simple Isabel!* (with pencil notes by another hand on 31<sup>v</sup>, 32<sup>v</sup>, 33<sup>v</sup>, 34<sup>v</sup>, 35<sup>v</sup>, 37<sup>v</sup>, 39<sup>v</sup>, 41<sup>v</sup>, 42<sup>v</sup>, 43<sup>v</sup>, 44<sup>v</sup>, 47<sup>v</sup>, 49<sup>v</sup>, 52<sup>v</sup>, 53<sup>v</sup>)

55<sup>v</sup>   Note on the next poem.

56<sup>r</sup>   *Hence Burgundy, Claret, and Port*

56<sup>r</sup>   *God of the Meridian*

57<sup>v</sup>   Note on the next poem.

58<sup>r</sup>   *No, those days are gone away*

60<sup>v</sup>   Note on the next poem.

61<sup>r</sup>   *Souls of poets dead and gone*

62<sup>r</sup>   *Not Aladdin magian*

64<sup>r</sup>   *When I have fears that I may cease to be* (notes on 63<sup>v</sup>)

65<sup>r</sup>   *Dear Reynolds, as last night I lay in bed* (notes on 65<sup>v</sup>, 66<sup>v</sup>)

68<sup>v</sup>   Note on the next poem.

69<sup>r</sup>   *Bards of passion and of mirth*

70<sup>v</sup>   Note on the next sonnet.

71<sup>r</sup>   *As Hermes once took to his feathers light*

71<sup>v</sup>   Note on the next poem.

72<sup>r</sup>   *O Goddess! hear these tuneless numbers, wrung* (notes on 73<sup>v</sup>)

75<sup>r</sup>   *And what is love?—it is a doll dress'd up* (notes on 74<sup>v</sup>)

75<sup>v</sup>   Note on the next poem.

76<sup>r</sup>   *O what can ail thee, knight at arms*

78<sup>r</sup>   *Standing aloof in giant ignorance*

78<sup>v</sup>   Note on the next poem.

79<sup>r</sup>   *Deep in the shady sadness of a vale* (notes on all versos of this text, except 95<sup>v</sup>, 97<sup>v</sup>, 98<sup>v</sup>, 101<sup>v</sup>, 105<sup>v</sup>)

109<sup>v</sup>   Note on the next poem.

110<sup>r</sup>   *Saint Agnes' Eve!—Ah, bitter chill it was* (notes on 110<sup>v</sup>, 111<sup>v</sup>, 114<sup>v</sup>, 119<sup>v</sup>, 121<sup>v</sup>, 122<sup>v</sup>, 123<sup>v</sup>)

124<sup>v</sup>   Note on the next poem.

125<sup>r</sup>   *Upon a Sabbath-day it fell* (note on 129<sup>v</sup>)

131<sup>r</sup>   *Hush, hush! tread softly! hush, hush my dear!*

131<sup>v</sup>   Note on the next poem.

132<sup>r</sup>   *Mother of Hermes! and still youthful Maia!*

133<sup>r</sup>   *Welcome joy, and welcome sorrow*

134<sup>r</sup>   *In short, convince you that however wise*

137<sup>r</sup>   *O were I one of the Olympian twelve*

139<sup>v</sup>   Note on the next sonnet.

140<sup>r</sup>   *Nature withheld Cassandra in the skies*

140<sup>v</sup>   Note on the next poem.

141   Excised.

142<sup>r</sup>   *Season of mists and mellow fruitfulness*

144<sup>r</sup>   *Spenser, a jealous honourer of thine*

144<sup>v</sup>   Note on the next poem.

145<sup>r</sup>   *Though you should build a bark of dead men's bones*

145<sup>r</sup>   *No, no, go not to Lethe, neither twist*

147<sup>r</sup>   *One morn before me were three figures seen* (notes on 146<sup>v</sup>, 147<sup>v</sup>, 148<sup>v</sup>)

150<sup>r</sup>   *He was to weet a melancholy carle*

151<sup>r</sup>   *O soft embalmer of the still midnight* (one word altered in the autograph of John Keats; notes on 150<sup>v</sup>)

152<sup>r</sup>   *Fame, like a wayward girl, will still be coy*

152<sup>v</sup>   Note on the next sonnet.

153<sup>r</sup>   *How fever'd is the man who cannot look*

154<sup>r</sup>   *If by dull rhymes our English must be chain'd*

154<sup>v</sup>   Note on the next poem.

155<sup>r</sup>   *Chief of organic numbers*

156<sup>v</sup>   Note on the next poem.

157$^r$   *My heart aches, and a drowsy numbness*
        *pains* (notes on 156$^v$, 159$^v$)

161$^r$   *Happy, happy, glowing fire*

165$^r$   *Fanatics have their dreams, wherewith they*
        *weave* (notes on all versos of this text,
        except 167$^v$, 171$^v$-177$^v$, 179$^v$)

182$^v$   Note on the next poem.

183$^r$   *Ever let the fancy roam*

187$^r$   *I had a dove, and the sweet dove died* and
        *Where's the Poet? Show him! show him!*

187$^v$   Note on the next poem.

188$^r$   *Thou still unravish'd bride of quietness*

190$^v$   Transcript in English of Boccaccio's story
        of Isabella.

193$^r$   *Come hither all sweet maidens soberly*

194$^r$   *Which of the fairest three*

195$^r$   *You say you love; but with a voice*

196$^r$   *In midmost Ind, beside Hydaspes cool*

212$^r$   *The day is gone, and all its sweets are gone*

212$^v$   Note on the next poem.

213$^r$   *There is a joy in footing slow across a silent*
        *plain*

215$^r$   *Four seasons fill the measure of the year*

216$^r$   *Oh Chatterton how very sad thy fate*

217$^r$   *Byron, how sweetly sad thy melody*

218$^r$   *O that a week could be an age, and we*

218$^v$   Note on the next poem.

219$^r$   *Stay, ruby breasted warbler, stay*

219$^r$   *O come, my dear Emma, the rose is full blown*

220$^r$   *O Peace! and dost thou with thy presence*
        *bless*

220$^v$   Note on the next poem.

221$^r$   *In thy western halls of gold*

222$^r$   *Fill for me a brimming bowl*

222$^v$   Note on the next poem.

223$^r$   *Hadst thou liv'd in days of old*
        (notes on 223$^v$)

234$^r$   Contents of this volume.

236$^v$   Original title, dedication, and preface to
        *Endymion.*

239$^v$   Alterations in *Endymion.*

240$^v$   Note on the inscription on the grave of
        Keats.

241$^r$   List by Woodhouse: "Poems of J. K.
        which I have not."

### 3.3
**Commonplace book of letters from John
Keats and others, compiled by Richard
Woodhouse;** transcripts by Woodhouse and by
others with revisions and corrections by
Woodhouse.

Brown unfinished sheep notebook, bookseller's
label inside back cover: "Sold by Black, Parry &
Kingsbury, 7 Leadenhall S$^t$." 84 leaves, 23.2 x 19
cm. Laid paper watermarked with fleur-de-lys
in crowned escutcheon and script initials
I. (or J.) F.

From the Crewe collection. Presented by Arthur A.
Houghton, Jr., 1970.

*Note*: this transcript is the sole authority for the text
of 15 letters from Keats to John Hamilton Reynolds,
one to John Taylor, and one to James Augustus
Hessey.

### Contents
*page*

1     Note in shorthand.

2     JK to John Taylor, 10 January 1818.
      Rollins 49.

3     JK to John Taylor, 30 January 1818.
      Rollins 57. Contains "Endymion,"
      I.777-781.

4     JK to John Taylor, 27 February 1818.
      Rollins 65.

6     JK to Taylor & Hessey, 21 March 1818.
      Rollins 71.

7   JK to John Taylor, 24 April 1818. Rollins 78. Contains proof revises for "Endymion."

9   JK to John Taylor, 21 June 1818. Rollins 88.

10  Notes by Richard Woodhouse on the public reception of "Endymion," including a letter signed J.S. in defense of the poem to the editor of the *Morning Chronicle*.

13  JK to J. A. Hessey, 8 October 1818. Rollins 110.

15  JK to Richard Woodhouse, 27 October 1818. Rollins 118.

17  Note by Woodhouse on the preceding letter; partially crossed out.

18  JK to John Hamilton Reynolds, 22 [?] September 1818. Rollins 108.

19  JK to Jane and Mariane Reynolds, 14 September 1817. Rollins 34.

23  JK to John Hamilton Reynolds, 19 February 1818. Rollins 62. Contains *O thou whose face hath felt the Winter's wind*.

25  Charles Brown to Woodhouse, 1 December 1818. Rollins 125.

26  Jane Porter to Henry Neville, 4 December 1818.

27  JK to Richard Woodhouse, 18 December 1818. Rollins 128.

28  JK to John Hamilton Reynolds, 3 February 1818. Rollins 59.

30  JK to John Hamilton Reynolds, 11 July 1819. Rollins 175.

31  JK to John Hamilton Reynolds, 24 August 1819. Rollins 185.

32  JK to John Taylor, 23 August 1819. Rollins 183.

33  JK to John Hamilton Reynolds, 21 September 1819. Rollins 193.

37  JK to John Taylor, 17 November 1819. Rollins 211.

38  JK to John Taylor, 31 August 1819. Rollins 188.

39  JK to John Taylor, 5 September 1819. Rollins 190.

42  JK to John Hamilton Reynolds, 17 March 1817. Rollins 18.

43  JK to John Hamilton Reynolds, 17–18 April 1817. Rollins 22.

46  JK to John Hamilton Reynolds, 21 September 1817. Rollins 36.

49  Benjamin Bailey to John Hamilton Reynolds, n.d. [1817].

49  JK to John Hamilton Reynolds, 9 March 1817. Rollins 16.

50  JK to John Hamilton Reynolds, 22 November 1817. Rollins 44. Contains "Endymion" IV.581-590.

53  JK to John Hamilton Reynolds, 31 January 1818. Rollins 58. Contains *O blush not so! O blush not so; Hence Burgundy, Claret, and Port; God of the Meridian*; and *When I have fears that I may cease to be*.

55  JK to John Hamilton Reynolds, 3 February 1818. Rollins 59. Beginning only, copied by mistake; already transcribed on p.28.

56  JK to John Hamilton Reynolds, 14 March 1818. Rollins 68.

58  JK to John Hamilton Reynolds, 9 April 1818. Rollins 76.

61  JK to John Hamilton Reynolds, 17 April 1818. Rollins 77.

62  JK to John Hamilton Reynolds, 27 April 1818. Rollins 79.

64  JK to John Hamilton Reynolds, 3 May 1818. Rollins 80. Contains *Mother of Hermes! and still youthful Maia*.

71  JK to John Hamilton Reynolds, 11–13 July 1818. Rollins 96.

74   JK to John Hamilton Reynolds,
25 March 1818. Rollins 74.

74   JK to Jane and Mariane Reynolds,
4 September 1817. Rollins 30.

76   JK to Benjamin Bailey,
8 October 1817. Rollins 38.

79   JK to Benjamin Bailey,
5 November 1817. Rollins 41.

80   JK to Benjamin Bailey,
22 November 1817. Rollins 43.

83   JK to Benjamin Bailey,
23 January 1818. Rollins 55.

86   JK to Benjamin Bailey,
21–25 May 1818. Rollins 83.

88   JK to Benjamin Bailey,
10 June 1818. Rollins 86.

90   JK to Benjamin Bailey,
18–22 July 1818. Rollins 99.

95   JK to Benjamin Bailey,
13 March 1818. Rollins 67. Contains
*Four seasons fill the measure of the year.*

99   JK to Benjamin Bailey,
14 August 1819. Rollins 181.

100   JK to Taylor & Hessey,
16 May 1817. Rollins 27.

101   JK to Taylor & Hessey,
10 June 1817. Rollins 28.

102   JK to "callers on John Taylor,"
January 1818 [?]. Rollins 47; and JK to John
Taylor, 23 January 1818. Rollins 54.

103   JK to John Taylor, 5 February 1818. Rollins
60; JK to John Taylor, 24 December 1818.
Rollins 133; and JK to Taylor & Hessey,
29 [?] May 1819. Rollins 163.

104   JK to John Taylor, 17 November 1819.
Rollins 211. Already copied above, p.37.

105   JK to John Taylor, 11 [?] June 1820.
Rollins 263; and JK to John Taylor,
13 August 1820. Rollins 279.

106   Richard Abbey to John Taylor,
18 April 1821. *KC* 114; and JK to James
Rice, 14–16 February 1820. Rollins 228.

108   JK to James Rice,
December 1819. Rollins 212.

111   JK to James Rice,
24 March 1818. Rollins 72.

113   JK to James Rice,
24 November 1818. Rollins 122.

155   "Mʳ Kean" [critique by Keats, differing
widely from the version printed in
*The Champion*, Sunday, 21 December 1817;
copied by a clerk with revisions by
Woodhouse. See Hampstead ed.,
V.227-232].

160   "Nominations" [a list of names with
proposers, with the results of election to
an unidentified group, beginning with J.
A. Hessey, nominated by John Taylor.]

### 3.4
**Scrapbook compiled by Georgiana Augusta
Wylie Keats and others.** Commonplace book
entries written in several hands, with mounted
newspaper cuttings and other ephemeral
material.

Green marbled boards with red morocco spine
and corners. 81 leaves, 22.3 x 18 cm. Mainly of
wove paper watermarked: C WILMOTT | 1810;
some leaves have been excised, others pasted
in. Most leaves were pasted over with cuttings,
manuscripts, and other items, frequently after
having been inscribed; where this covered
significant text, they were removed by H.
Buxton Forman, and are preserved in a
separate folder. In Garrod's edition, assigned
the siglum a; in Stillinger's edition, GAW.

Maurice S. Gollancz (March 1880); Robson &
Kerslake, booksellers, London. H. Buxton Forman;
Maurice Buxton Forman; Frank Sykes (sale,
Sotheby, 23 June 1947, lot 220c). Presented by Arthur
A. Houghton, Jr., 1968.

CONTENTS

*(only pages containing Keatsiana are listed, with a note on the handwriting of each)*

*folio*

In addition, the notebook contains the "Monody on the death of Mr. T. B. Sheridan," beginning *Yes, grief will have way, but the fast falling tear,* by Thomas Moore, transcribed once by Georgiana Keats (3ʳ) and once by George Keats (37ʳ), and annotated by Georgiana Keats: "from MSS of J. Keats August 1816."

**3.5**

**Commonplace book compiled by Tom Keats, signed twice by him and once by John Keats; July–August 1814.**

Marbled paper wrappers. 12 leaves, 21.9 x 18.3 cm. Wove paper watermarked: C WILMOTT | 1814. In Garrod's edition, assigned the siglum b; in Stillinger's, TK.

Tom Keats; George Scott; George Allison Armour. Presented by Arthur A. Houghton, Jr., 1970.

CONTENTS

*page*

**3.6**

**Transcripts by Charles Brown of poems by John Keats, revised in several places by Keats and with some annotations by Richard Monckton Milnes.** Evidently used in part as a printer's copy for *Life, Letters, and Literary Remains* (1848), II, 109ff., with some compositors' names noted. Reconstituted by Mabel A. E. Steele from elements in the two sets of transcripts designated in Garrod as T and T2; in Stillinger's edition, CB.

Unbound. 31 leaves, 22 x 18 cm. Wove paper watermarked: S & C WISE | 1815. Variously foliated and paged: the official pagination is in red pencil in the lower right corners of the pages.

Same provenance as 1.14. Presented by Arthur A. Houghton, Jr., 1970.

Published in facsimile in *The Charles Brown Poetry Transcripts at Harvard*, ed. by Jack Stillinger; volume 7 of *The Manuscripts of the Younger Romantics* (New York, 1988), pp. 3-64.

CONTENTS

**3.7**

**Transcript by Charles Brown of *Otho the Great*, with autograph revisions by John Keats in numerous places.** Used as printers' copy for *Life, Letters, and Literary Remains* (1848).

Bound in modern russet morocco. 116p. on 105 leaves, 22.5 x 18.2 cm., lacking the original f.1 (containing I.i.1-18). Wove paper unwatermarked, some leaves embossed in upper left with rectangular die of a crown and the name BATH.

Same provenance as 1.14. Presented by Arthur A. Houghton, Jr., 1970.

Published in facsimile in *The Charles Brown Poetry Transcripts at Harvard*, ed. by Jack Stillinger; volume 7 of *The Manuscripts of the Younger Romantics* (New York, 1988), pp. 73-191.

**3.8**

**Transcript by Tom Keats of *I stood tip-toe upon a little hill*; here headed "Endymion" (its original title).**

Unbound. 8p. on 4 leaves, probably formerly two conjugate pairs quired one inside the other, 24.6 x 18.9 cm. Laid paper watermarked with triple plume on a coronet, and MOLINEUX & JOHNSTON. This paper is the same as or closely similar to that of the complete autograph copy (2.9). Garrod wrongly states that it is from Tom Keats's copy-book, which is on different paper.

H. Buxton Forman (who wrongly identified the transcriber as George Keats). Presented by Arthur A. Houghton, Jr., 1970.

**3.9**

**Transcripts by John Jeffrey of letters of John Keats.**

Unbound. 59p. on 30 leaves, 32.3 x 19 cm. Ruled wove paper unwatermarked. Jeffrey arbitrarily omitted large portions of the letters, but his

transcripts provide the only authority for the text of six letters. Jeffrey made his transcripts in 1845; see note on 1.22.

Same provenance as 1.14. Presented by Arthur A. Houghton, Jr., 1970.

CONTENTS

*folio*

Contains *Why did I laugh tonight? No voice will tell*; *He is to weet a melancholy carle*; *As Hermes once took to his feathers light*; and *If by dull rhymes our English must be chained*.

27ᵛ   JK to George and Georgiana Keats,
      17–27 September 1819. Rollins 199.

29ʳ   JK to Georgiana Keats,
      13–28 January 1820. Rollins 215.

## 3.10
### Miscellaneous transcripts by several hands of poems and letters by John Keats.

Unbound.

Same provenance as 1.14. Presented by Arthur A. Houghton, Jr., 1970.

### POEMS

*item*

(1)   *The church-bells toll a melancholy round*; and *Highmindedness, a jealousy for good*

      Unidentified hand. 2p. on 1 leaf, 22.5 x 18.3 cm. Laid paper watermarked with a fleur-de-lys and script initials: W D W.

(2)   *I stood tip-toe upon a little hill*; lines 61-64, 111-114 only, plus 4 cancelled lines.

      Transcript by W. H. Prideaux. 1p. on 1 leaf, 20.2 x 11.5 cm. Blue wove paper unwatermarked.

(3)   *I had a dove and the sweet dove died*

      Transcript by Richard Monckton Milnes. 1p. on 1 leaf, 22.5 x 18.5 cm. Wove paper unwatermarked.

(4)   *Shed no tear—O shed no tear*

      Transcript by Richard Monckton Milnes. 1p. on 1 leaf, 22.7 x 17.8 cm. Bluish wove paper unwatermarked.

(5)   *Why did I laugh tonight? No voice will tell*

      Transcript by Richard Monckton Milnes. 1p. on 1 leaf, 22.3 x 18.2 cm. Wove paper watermarked: J WHATMAN | TURKEY MILL

| 1847; oval embossed stamp on upper left corner, crown and the words: LONDON SUPERFINE.

(6)   *Physician Nature! Let my spirit blood*

      Transcript by Richard Monckton Milnes. 4p. on 2 conjugate leaves, 22.9 x 18.4 cm. Bluish wove paper unwatermarked.

(7)   *Oh! how I love, on a fair summer's eve*

      Transcript by Coventry Patmore. 1p. on 1 leaf, 23 x 18.3 cm. Bluish wove paper unwatermarked.

(8)   *Fresh morning gusts have blown away all fear*

      Transcript by Coventry Patmore. 1p. on 1 leaf, 23 x 18.3 cm. Same paper as (7).

(9)   *Blue!—Tis the life of Heaven—the domain*

      Transcript by Coventry Patmore. 1p. on 1 leaf, 23 x 18.3 cm. Same paper as (7).

(10)  *O that a week could be an age, and we*

      Transcript by Coventry Patmore. 1p. on 1 leaf, 23 x 18.2 cm. Same paper as (7).

(11)  *Time's sea hath been five years at its slow ebb*

      Transcript by Coventry Patmore. 1p. on 1 leaf, 23 x 18.5 cm. Same paper as (7).

(12)  *After dark vapours have oppressed our plains*

      Transcribed by Coventry Patmore. 1p. on 1 leaf, 23 x 18.3 cm. Same paper as (7).

(13)  *This pleasant tale is like a little copse*

      Transcript by Coventry Patmore. 1p. on 1 leaf, 23 x 18.2 cm. Same paper as (7).

(14)  *It keeps eternal whisperings around*

      Transcript by Coventry Patmore. 1p. on 1 leaf, 23 x 18.4 cm. Same paper as (7).

(15)  *Stay, ruby breasted warbler, stay*

      Transcript by Coventry Patmore. 2p. on 2 leaves, 23 x 18.2 cm. Same paper as (7).

(16)  *As from the darkening gloom a silver dove*

      Transcript by Coventry Patmore. 1p. on 1 leaf, 23 x 17.9 cm. Same paper as (7).

(17)  *Four seasons fill the measure of the year*
Transcript by Coventry Patmore. 1p. on
1 leaf, 22.8 x 17.8 cm. Same paper as (7).

(18)  *Spenser! a jealous honourer of thine*
Transcript by W. A. Longmore from
original MS. in scrapbook of his mother,
Eliza Reynolds Longmore. 1p. on 1 leaf,
17.9 x 22.2 cm. Laid paper watermarked:
[script] W N | SUPERFINE.

(19)  *As Hermes once took to his feather light*;
*Fame like a wayward girl will still be coy*;
and *'Tis the witching time of night*
Transcript by John Howard Payne. 3p. on
2 conjugate leaves, 26.5 x 20.1 cm. Wove
paper unwatermarked.

Includes transcript of letter from George
Keats to Payne, Louisville, Kentucky,
1834, transmitting the texts which George
had copied from JK's letters.

LETTERS

(20)  JK to Charles Brown,
15 May 1820. Rollins 260.

Transcript by Coventry Patmore. 1p. on
1 leaf, 23 x 18.8 cm. Same paper as (7).

(21)  JK to Charles Wentworth Dilke,
20–21 September 1818. Rollins 107.

Transcript by Coventry Patmore. 5p. on
2 conjugate and 3 separate leaves, 24.5 x
19.8 cm. Same paper as (7).

(22)  JK to John Hamilton Reynolds,
17 March 1817. Rollins 18.

Transcript by Coventry Patmore. 1p. on
1 leaf, 22.9 x 18.6 cm. Laid paper
watermarked: J WHATMAN; probably
same paper as (23).

(23)  JK to John Hamilton Reynolds,
17–18 April 1817. Rollins 22.

Transcript by Coventry Patmore. 5p. on
2 pairs of conjugate leaves and 1 single

leaf, 22.9 x 18.6 cm. Laid paper
watermarked: J WHATMAN | TURKEY MILL
| 1845. Contains *It keeps eternal
whisperings around.*

(24)  JK to George and Tom Keats,
5 January 1818 (wrongly transcribed as
5 April). Rollins 48.

Transcript by Coventry Patmore. 4p. on
2 conjugate and 2 separate leaves, 24 x
19.6 cm. Bluish wove paper
unwatermarked.

(25)  JK to Benjamin Bailey,
8 October 1817. Rollins 38.

Transcript by Coventry Patmore. 3p. on
2 conjugate leaves and 1 separate leaf,
22.9 x 18.6 cm. Same paper as (23).

(26)  JK to Tom Keats,
17–21 July 1818. Rollins 98.

Unidentified hand. 4p. on 4 leaves, 32.2 x
19.7 cm. Laid paper watermarked:
W TUCKER | 1842.

Contains *All gentle folk who owe a grudge*;
and *Of late two dainties were before me
plac'd.*

(27)  JK To James Rice,
14–16 February 1820. Rollins 228.

Unidentified hand. 4p. on 2 conjugate
leaves, 24 x 20.2 cm. Blue laid paper
watermarked: R BARNARD | 1861, with
countermark of lion within a crowned
oval.

(28)  JK to John Hamilton Reynolds,
24 August 1819. Rollins 185.

Unidentified hand. 2p. on 2 leaves, 31.8 x
20 cm. Blue laid paper watermarked with
seated Britannia in a crowned oval.

(29)  JK to John Taylor, 10 January 1818.
Rollins 49; JK to John Taylor,
23 January 1818. Rollins 54.

Unidentified hand. 2p. on 2 conjugate
leaves, 32.2. x 20.2 cm. Same paper as (27).

(30) JK to John Taylor, 17 November 1819.
Rollins 211; JK to John Taylor,
13 August 1820. Rollins 279.

Unidentified hand. 3p. on 2 conjugate
leaves, 32.2 x 20.2 cm. Same paper as (27).

Items (27) to (30) in same hand as in Keats
*EC8.K2262.W848ma v.I, Benjamin
Robert Haydon to John Keats,
[21 March 1818].

PROSE TRANSCRIPTS

(31) Article on Edmund Kean, from *The
Champion*, 21 December 1817.

Transcript by Coventry Patmore. 6p. on
6 leaves, 24.5 x 18.5 cm. Blue wove paper
unwatermarked.

(32) Review of *Rob Roy* at Drury Lane
Theatre, from *The Champion*,
30 March 1818.

Transcript by Coventry Patmore. 10p. on
4 pairs of conjugate and 2 single leaves,
24.5 x 18.5 cm. Same paper as (31).

(33) Review of *Marquis de Carabas* at Covent
Garden, from *The Champion*, 5 April 1818.

Transcript by Coventry Patmore. 4p. on
2 pairs of conjugate leaves, 24.5 x 18.5 cm.
Same paper as (31).

(34) Article on Drury Lane, from
*The Champion*, 7 December 1818.

Transcript by Coventry Patmore. 12p. on
1 pair of conjugate and 10 single leaves,
24.5 x 18.5 cm. Same paper as (31).

(35) Review of Edmund Kean as Richard III,
from *The Champion*, 28 December 1817.

Transcript by Coventry Patmore. 12p. on
12 leaves, 23 x 18.8 cm. Bluish paper
unwatermarked.

### 3.11

**Transcript by Charles Brown of *King Stephen*,
I.i.l to I.ii.19a.**

Unbound. 6p. on 3 leaves, 22 x 18.3 cm. Wove
paper unwatermarked. This manuscript
together with the portion in Keats's hand (2.28)
comprises the whole text of this fragmentary
work.

Same provenance as 1.14. Presented by Arthur A.
Houghton, Jr., 1970.

Published in facsimile in *The Charles Brown Poetry
Transcripts at Harvard*, ed. by Jack Stillinger; volume
7 of *The Manuscripts of the Younger Romantics* (New
York, 1988), pp. 65-70.

### 3.12

**Poems by John Keats with several, never yet
published. . . . London, written by J. C.
Stephens for I[sabella] J[ane] Towers. 1828.**

Notebook bound in russet morocco gilt. 130p.
on 70 leaves, 17.8 x 10.8 cm. Wove paper
watermarked: G & R TURNER | 1827.

Same provenance as 1.14. Presented by Arthur A.
Houghton, Jr., 1970.

From f.3ʳ to f.65ᵛ, transcribed from a copy of *Poems*
(1817); the remaining texts transcribed from manu-
script sources.

CONTENTS

*folio*

25ᵛ   *Now morning from her orient chamber came*

27ʳ   *Woman! when I behold thee flippant, vain*

27ᵛ   *Light foot, dark violet eyes, and parted hair*

28ʳ   *Ah! who can e'er forget so fair a being?*

30ʳ   *Sweet are the pleasures that to verse belong*

33ʳ   *Full many a dreary hour have I past*

37ᵛ   *Oft have you seen a swan superbly frowning*

43ʳ   *Many the wonders I this day have seen*

43ᵛ   *Had I a man's fair form, then might my sighs*

44ʳ   *What tho' for shewing truth to flatter'd state*

44ᵛ   *How many bards gild the lapses of time!*

45ʳ   *As late I rambled in the happy fields*

45ᵛ   *Nymph of the downward smile and sidelong glance*

46ʳ   *Oh solitude! if I must with thee dwell*

46ᵛ   *Small busy flames play thro' the fresh laid coals*

47ʳ   *Keen fitful gusts are whispering here & there*

47ᵛ   *To one who has been long in city pent*

48ʳ   *Much have I travelled in the realms of gold*

48ᵛ   *Give me a golden pen & let me lean*

49ʳ   *Highmindedness, a jealousy for good*

49ᵛ   *Great spirits now on earth are sojourning*

50ʳ   *The poetry of Earth is never dead*

50ᵛ   *Good Kosciusko, thy great name alone*

51ʳ   *Happy is England! I could be content*

53ʳ   *What is more gentle than a wind in summer?*

66ʳ   *Come hither all sweet maidens soberly*

66ᵛ   *Four Seasons fill the measure of the year*

67ʳ   *Hearken thou craggy ocean pyramid!*

67ᵛ   *Welcome Joy, and welcome sorrow*

69ʳ   *The church bells toll a melancholy round*

69ᵛ   *Before he went to feed with owls and bats*

70ʳ   *This pleasant tale is like a little copse*
(transcript by Isabella Jane Towers)

70ᵛ   *In a drear-nighted December* (transcript added by Isabella Jane Towers)

### 3.13

**Commonplace book of verse and prose by various authors, compiled by William Pitter Woodhouse; July–August 1827.** Mostly in Woodhouse's autograph, with a few words written by his brother, Richard Woodhouse.

Two russet calf notebooks; stamped in gilt at foot of spine: I. THOMAS & Cᵒ. | 20 Cornhill | PATENT. V.1, 82 leaves, faintly ruled, 19.1 x 12.5 cm. V.2, 129 leaves, identical ruling and size. Wove paper unwatermarked.

Seen and quoted by Sir Sidney Colvin, *Times Literary Supplement*, 18 February 1915, p.56.

Purchased from Raphael King through the gift of Arthur A. Houghton, Jr., 1949.

### CONTENTS

*(only pages containing Keatsiana are listed; the notebooks also contain a few selections from John Hamilton Reynolds, James Rice, and John Taylor)*

I, f.25ᵛ   *In drear-nighted December*
(widely variant third stanza)

II, f.3ᵛ   *Nymph of the downward smile and sidelong glance*

Pisa — July 27, 1820.

My dear Keats

I hear with great pain the dangerous accident that you have undergone, & Mr Gisborne who gives me the account of it, adds, that you continue to wear a consumptive appearance. This consumption is a disease particularly fond of people who write such good verses as you have done, and with the assistance of an English winter it can often indulge its selection;— I do not think that young & amiable poets are at all bound to gratify its taste; they have entered into no bond with the Muses to that effect... But seriously (for I am joking on what I am very anxious about) I think you would do well to pass the winter 
endure an accident in Italy. If you think it as necessary as I do, so long as you could 
Pisa or its neighbourhood agreeth to you, Mrs Shelley unites with myself in urging the request, that you would take up your residence with us.— You might come by sea to Leghorn, (Rome is not worth seeing, & the sea air is particularly good for weak lungs) which is within a few miles of us. You ought at all events to see Italy, & your health which I suggest as a motive, might be an excuse to you.— I spare declamation about the statues & the paintings & the ruins — & what is a greater piece of forbearance, about the mountains the streams & the fields, the colours of the sky, & the sky itself.—

I have lately read your Endymion again & even with a new sense of the treasures of poetry it contains, tho' treasures poured forth with indistinct profusion. This, people in general will not forgive, & that is the cause of the comparatively few copies which have been sold. — I feel persuaded that you are capable of the greatest things, so you but will.

4.17.1.

PERCY BYSSHE SHELLEY. Autograph letter signed to John Keats, 27 July 1820 (MS Keats 4.17.1)
Bequest of Amy Lowell

# IV. KEATS'S CIRCLE

*Materials in this section are listed in MS Keats number sequence. Included under each name heading are (in this order): letters from and to, including transcripts (interfiled chronologically); manuscripts; and, occasionally, material about the person. Family members are grouped together, even if their last names differ (e.g. Clarke); thus, the arrangement of entries is not strictly alphabetical. For a complete listing of material by a particular author, consult the Name Index (pp. 119-120).*

### Aitken, John, 1793–1833.

**4.1.1**    A.L.s. to [John Keats]; East Lothian Bank, Dunbar, 17 August 1820. Rollins 286.

4p. on 2 conjugate leaves, 25.2 x 20.1 cm. Wove paper watermarked: IPING | 1813.

Bequeathed by Amy Lowell, 1925.

### Bailey, Benjamin, 1791?–1853.

**4.2.1**    A.L.s. (draft, not sent) to [Richard Monckton Milnes, Baron Houghton]; Ratnapoora, Ceylon, 7 May 1849. See *KC* 253.

51p. on 12 pairs of conjugate leaves and 2 single leaves, 24.1 x 18.7 cm. and smaller. Bluish laid paper watermarked: EDWARD SMITH | 1847, with countermark of crowned fleur-de-lys and script initials E S.

Presented by Arthur A. Houghton, Jr., 1970.

This draft contains much revision; a fair transcript by Bailey's daughter (4.2.2) was actually sent to

Milnes, and is the text reprinted in *KC*. Contains Bailey's reminiscences of Keats.

**4.2.2**    MS.L.s. (in the hand of Bailey's daughter, with his autograph revisions) to [Richard Monckton Milnes, Baron Houghton]; Ratnapoora, Ceylon, 7 May 1849. *KC* 253.

68p. on 17 pairs of conjugate leaves, 25.8 x 20 cm. Bluish wove paper unwatermarked.

Same provenance as 1.14. Presented by Arthur A. Houghton, Jr., 1970.

**4.2.3**    MS.L. (transcript, unidentified hand) to the Editor of the Oxford Herald; [n.p.] 30 May, 6 June 1818.

19p. on 10 pairs of conjugate leaves, 32.4 x 20 cm. Blue laid paper watermarked: KENT, with countermark of seated Britannia in a crowned oval.

Same provenance as 1.14. Presented by Arthur A. Houghton, Jr., 1970.

These letters, signed "N.Y.," are tantamount to a review of Keats's poems.

**4.2.4**    A.L.s. to John Taylor; Burton-on-Trent, 2 April 1824. *KC* 339.

4p. on 2 conjugate leaves, 23 x 18.7 cm. Laid paper watermarked: S E & Cº | 1819. Red wax seal.

Presented by Donald P. Perry, 1947.

**4.2.5**    A.L.s. to John Taylor; Burton-on-Trent, 10 May 1824. *KC* 134.

4p. on 2 conjugate leaves, 23 x 18.7 cm. Same paper as 4.2.4. Red wax seal.

Same provenance as 4.2.4.

**4.2.6**    A.L.s. to John Taylor; Burton-on-Trent, 9 June 1824. *KC* 340.

4p. on 2 conjugate leaves, 23 x 18.7 cm. Same paper as 4.2.4. Remains of red wax seal.

Same provenance as 4.2.4.

**4.2.7**    A.L.s. to John Taylor; Burton-on-Trent, 14 June 1824. *KC* 342.

4p. on 2 conjugate leaves, 23 x 18.9 cm. Laid paper watermarked with crowned posthorn and script initials R B. Red wax seal.

Same provenance as 4.2.4.

**4.2.8**    A.L.s. to [Richard Monckton Milnes, Baron Houghton]; Colombo, Ceylon, 15 October 1848. *KC* 251.

8p. on 2 conjugate leaves and 2 single leaves, 24.8 x 20 cm. and smaller. White and blue wove paper unwatermarked.

Same provenance as 1.14. Presented by Arthur A. Houghton, Jr., 1970.

**4.2.9**    A.L.s. to [Richard Monckton Milnes, Baron Houghton]; Colombo, Ceylon, 11 May 1849. *KC* 254.

4p. on 2 conjugate leaves, 23 x 18.3 cm. Wove paper unwatermarked.

Same provenance as 1.14. Presented by Arthur A. Houghton, Jr., 1970.

**4.2.10**    A.L.s. to [John Taylor]; Colombo, Ceylon, 13 August 1849. *KC* 257.

4p. on 2 conjugate leaves, 19 x 12.1 cm. Blue wove paper unwatermarked.

Same provenance as 4.2.4.

**4.2.11**    A.L.s. to [Richard Monckton Milnes, Baron Houghton]; Ratnapoora, Ceylon, 11 September 1849. *KC* 258.

4p. on 2 conjugate leaves, 20 x 12.6 cm. Blue wove paper unwatermarked.

Same provenance as 1.14. Presented by Arthur A. Houghton, Jr., 1970.

**4.2.12**    Milnes, Richard Monckton, Baron Houghton, 1809-1885. Verses on the supposed death of Benjamin Bailey. *KC* 259.

A.MS. unsigned; [n.p., 1849?]

1p. on slip of paper, 5.3 x 17.1 cm. Wove paper unwatermarked. Formerly attached to 4.2.11.

Same provenance as 1.14. Presented by Arthur A. Houghton, Jr., 1970.

### Brown, Charles Armitage, 1786–1842.

**4.3.1**    A.L.s. to Richard Woodhouse; Hampstead, 1 December [1818]. *KC* 28. Rollins 125.

2p. on 2 conjugate leaves, 18.4 x 11.2 cm. Wove paper watermarked: J GREEN | 1818. Black wax seal.

Bequeathed by Amy Lowell, 1925.

Tells of the death of Tom Keats.

**4.3.2**    A.L.s. to William Haslam; Chichester, 30 September 1821. *KC* 72.

2p. on 1 leaf, 23.4 x 18.7 cm. Laid paper unwatermarked. Red wax seal.

Same provenance as 1.14. Presented by Arthur A. Houghton, Jr., 1970.

**4.3.3**    A.L.s. to William Haslam; Hampstead, 1 December 1820. *KC* 81.

2p. on 1 leaf, 22.6 x 18.2 cm. Wove paper watermarked: 1818. Red wax seal.

Same provenance as 1.14. Presented by Arthur A. Houghton, Jr., 1970.

**4.3.4**    A.L.s. to William Haslam; Hampstead, [10?] December 1820. *KC* 83.

2p. on 1 leaf, 22.6 x 18.2 cm. Same paper as 4.3.3. Red wax seal.

Same provenance as 1.14. Presented by Arthur A. Houghton, Jr., 1970.

**4.3.5**    A.L.s. to John Keats; Hampstead, 21 December 1820. Rollins 312.

4p. on 2 conjugate leaves, 22.6 x 18.3 cm. Same paper as 4.3.3.

Lucius Wilmerding. Presented by Arthur A. Houghton, Jr., 1970.

**4.3.6**    A.L.s. to William Haslam; Hampstead, 5 January 1821. *KC* 88.

2p. on 2 conjugate leaves, 22.7 x 18.9 cm. Same paper as 4.3.3. Red wax seal.

Same provenance as 1.14. Presented by Arthur A. Houghton, Jr., 1970.

**4.3.7**    A.L.s. to Joseph Severn; Hampstead, 15 January 1821. See *KC* 93.

4p. on 2 conjugate leaves, 22.7 x 18.3 cm. Same paper as 4.3.3. Pen sketches by Severn on p.4.

Presented by Arthur A. Houghton, Jr., 1954.

Printed in *KC* from a transcript (4.3.8).

**4.3.8**    MS.L. (transcript of 4.3.7, unidentified hand). *KC* 93.

2p. on 1 leaf, 24.2 x 19.8 cm. Wove paper unwatermarked.

Same provenance as 1.14. Presented by Arthur A. Houghton, Jr., 1970.

**4.3.9**    A.L.s. to Joseph Severn; Hampstead, 30 January 1821.

3p. on 2 conjugate leaves, 22.7 x 18.3 cm. Same paper as 4.3.3.

Same provenance as 4.3.7.

**4.3.10**    A.L.s. to Taylor & Hessey; Hampstead, [17 March 1821]. *KC* 108.

2p. on 1 leaf, 22.7 x 18.3. Same paper as 4.3.3.

Same provenance as 1.14. Presented by Arthur A. Houghton, Jr., 1970.

**4.3.11**    A.L.s. to William Haslam; Hampstead, 18 March [1821]. *KC* 111.

2p. on 2 conjugate leaves, 18.5 x 11.4 cm. Same paper as 4.3.3. Black wax seal.

Same provenance as 1.14. Presented by Arthur A. Houghton, Jr., 1970.

Tells of the death of John Keats.

**4.3.12**    A.L.s. to Joseph Severn; Hampstead, 23 March 1821.

4p. on 2 conjugate leaves, 22.7 x 18.3 cm. Same paper as 4.3.3. Pen sketches by Severn on p.4.

Same provenance as 4.3.7.

**4.3.13**    A.L.s. to Joseph Severn; Pisa, 5 September 1822.

4p. on 2 conjugate leaves, 24.5 x 19.8 cm. Wove paper watermarked: J GREEN | 1815. Red wax seal.

Same provenance as 4.3.7.

**4.3.14**    A.L.s. to Joseph Severn; Pisa, 23 September 1822.

2p. on 1 leaf, 24.9 x 17.9 cm. Laid paper unwatermarked. Red wax seal.

Same provenance as 4.3.7.

**4.3.15**    A.L.s. to Joseph Severn; Florence, 8 September 1824.

4p. on 2 conjugate leaves, 25.6 x 21 cm. Wove paper unwatermarked.

Same provenance as 4.3.7.

**4.3.16**    A.L.s. to Joseph Severn; Florence, 3 October 1832.

4p. on 2 conjugate leaves, 24.4. x 18.5 cm. Wove paper unwatermarked.

Same provenance as 4.3.7.

**4.3.17**    A.L.s. to Joseph Severn; Laira Green, 6 July 1835.

4p. on 2 conjugate leaves, 23.4 x 18.8 cm. Laid paper watermarked: W H SMITH | 192 STRAND.

Same provenance as 4.3.7.

**4.3.18**   A.L. (latter portion with signature wanting) to Leigh Hunt; Laira Green, 21 December 1836. *KC* 154.

2p. on 1 leaf, 23.3 x 18.6 cm. Wove paper unwatermarked.

Presented by Arthur A. Houghton, Jr., 1970.

Concerns the writing of Brown's life of Keats.

**4.3.19**   A.L.s. to Joseph Severn; Laira Green, 23 August 1838.

4p. on 2 conjugate leaves, 23.3 x 18.5 cm. Same paper as 4.3.17.

Same provenance as 4.3.7.

On the life of Keats, and the possibility of publishing the posthumous poems.

**4.3.20**   A.L.s. to Richard Monckton Milnes, Baron Houghton; Laira Green, [18] October 1840. *KC* 160.

2p. on 2 conjugate leaves, 22.2 x 18.6 cm. Wove paper watermarked: T Nash. Red wax seal.

Same provenance as 1.40. Presented by Arthur A. Houghton, Jr., 1970.

**4.3.21**   A.L.s. to [Richard Monckton Milnes, Baron Houghton]; Laira Green, 25 October 1840. *KC* 161.

4p. on 2 conjugate leaves, 22.2 x 18.6 cm. Same paper as 4.3.20.

Same provenance as 1.14. Presented by Arthur A. Houghton, Jr., 1970.

**4.3.22**   A.L.s. to Richard Monckton Milnes, Baron Houghton; Laira Green, 14 March 1841. *KC* 164.

3p. on 2 conjugate leaves, 22.2 x 18.6 cm. Same paper as 4.3.20.

Same provenance as 1.14. Presented by Arthur A. Houghton, Jr., 1970.

**4.3.23**   A.L.s. to Richard Monckton Milnes, Baron Houghton; Laira Green, 19 March 1841. *KC* 165.

3p. on 2 conjugate leaves, 22.2 x 18.6 cm. Same paper as 4.3.20.

Same provenance as 1.14. Presented by Arthur A. Houghton, Jr., 1970.

**4.3.24**   A.L.s. to [Richard Monckton Milnes, Baron Houghton]; Laira Green, 29 March 1841. *KC* 168.

4p. on 2 conjugate leaves, 22.2 x 18.6 cm. Same paper as 4.3.20.

Same provenance as 1.14. Presented by Arthur A. Houghton, Jr., 1970.

**4.3.25**   A.L.s. to Richard Monckton Milnes, Baron Houghton; Laira Green, 9 April 1841. *KC* 169.

4p. on 2 conjugate leaves, 22.2 x 18.6 cm. Same paper as 4.3.20.

Same provenance as 1.14. Presented by Arthur A. Houghton, Jr., 1970.

**4.3.26**   *Far down in the lowland of Scotland* (40 lines of verse)

MS. (in the hand of Charles Cowden Clarke); [n.p., n.d.].

2p. on 1 leaf, 25 x 20.4 cm. Wove paper unwatermarked.

A mildly indecent rhyme ascribed by Clarke to Charles Armitage Brown.

**4.3.27**   Life of John Keats.

A.MS.s.; [n.p., 1836-1840]. *KC* 166.

50p. on 46 leaves, 25.1 x 18.3 cm. Wove paper unwatermarked.

Same provenance as 1.14. Presented by Arthur A. Houghton, Jr., 1970.

Contains Brown's transcripts of nine letters of Keats, of which only one original has survived: 22 September 1819, Rollins 195; 23 September 1819, Rollins 197; 15 May 1819, Rollins 260; ca. 21 June 1820, Rollins 266; 14 August 1820, Rollins 284; August [?] 1820, Rollins 288; 28 September 1820, Rollins 302; 1 November 1820, Rollins 306; 30 November 1820, Rollins 310.

*Clarke, Charles Cowden, 1787–1877.*

**4.4.1**    A.L.s. to Joseph Severn; [London], 15 March 1831.

4p. on 2 conjugate leaves, 23.1 x 18.8 cm. Wove paper unwatermarked.

On p.3, a note to Severn from Vincent Novello; on p.4, a note to Severn from Mary Sabilla Novello.

Same provenance as 4.3.7.

**4.4.2**    A.L.s. to Richard Monckton Milnes, Baron Houghton; [London], 17 March 1846. *KC* 188.

3p. on 2 conjugate leaves, 25 x 20.4 cm. Wove paper unwatermarked.

Once accompanied 4.4.18.

Same provenance as 1.14. Presented by Arthur A. Houghton, Jr., 1970.

**4.4.3**    A.L.s. to Richard Monckton Milnes, Baron Houghton; [London], 17 March 1846. *KC* 189.

4p. on 2 conjugate leaves, 25 x 20.4 cm. Same paper as 4.4.2.

Same provenance as 1.14. Presented by Arthur A. Houghton, Jr., 1970.

**4.4.4**    Transcripts by Charles Cowden Clarke of poems by Keats: *Think not of it, sweet one, so; Unfelt, unheard, unseen; Welcome joy, and welcome sorrow.*

5p. on 3 leaves, 25 x 20.4 cm. Same paper as 4.4.2.

Once accompanied 4.4.3.

Same provenance as 1.14. Presented by Arthur A. Houghton, Jr., 1970.

**4.4.5**    A.L.s. to Richard Monckton Milnes, Baron Houghton; Stratford on Avon, 26 March 1846. *KC* 190.

2p. on 2 conjugate leaves, 21 x 13.2 cm. Bluish wove paper unwatermarked.

Same provenance as 1.14. Presented by Arthur A. Houghton, Jr., 1970.

**4.4.6**    A.L.s. to Richard Monckton Milnes, Baron Houghton; [London], 20 December 1846. *KC* 202.

4p. on 2 conjugate leaves, 20.6 x 12.5 cm. Wove paper unwatermarked.

Same provenance as 1.14. Presented by Arthur A. Houghton, Jr., 1970.

**4.4.7**    A.L.s. to Richard Monckton Milnes, Baron Houghton; [London], 26 December 1846. *KC* 205.

1p. on 2 conjugate leaves, 21 x 13.3 cm. Bluish wove paper unwatermarked.

Same provenance as 1.14. Presented by Arthur A. Houghton, Jr., 1970.

**4.4.8**    A.L.s. to Richard Monckton Milnes, Baron Houghton; [London], 7-12 August 1848. *KC* 236.

4p. on 2 conjugate leaves, 19.3 x 12 cm. Bluish wove paper unwatermarked; embossed with bust of Shakespeare.

Same provenance as 1.14. Presented by Arthur A. Houghton, Jr., 1970.

**4.4.9**    A.L.s. to [name excised]; Genoa, 16 March 1863.

4p. on 2 conjugate leaves, 18.2 x 11.2 cm. Laid paper watermarked with crowned posthorn; same embossed stamp as 4.4.8.

Presented by Arthur A. Houghton, Jr., 1951.

**4.4.10**    MS.L.s. (in hand of Mary Cowden Clarke, who also signed it) to James Thomas Fields; Genoa, 13 June 1873.

2p. on 1 leaf, 26.3 x 21.7 cm. Wove paper unwatermarked, with printed map of Genoa as letterhead.

Louis Holman collection. Purchased with funds presented by Arthur A. Houghton Jr., 1940.

**4.4.11**   A.L.s. to Clara [Novello];
[Genoa?], 3 May 1875.

2p. on 1 leaf, 21 x 13.4 cm. Laid paper
unwatermarked.

Same provenance as 4.3.7.

**4.4.12**   A.L.s. to Joseph Severn;
Genoa, 2 June 1875.

3p. on 2 conjugate leaves, 21.2 x 13.5 cm. Wove
paper watermarked with horizontal parallel
lines; same embossed stamp as 4.4.8.

Same provenance as 4.3.7.

### Clarke, Mary Cowden, 1809–1898.

**4.4.13**   A.L.s. to Joseph Severn;
Genoa, 27 November 1877.

2p. on 1 leaf of mourning paper, 20.9 x 13.5 cm.
Laid paper watermarked: VILALON; same
embossed stamp as 4.4.8.

Same provenance as 4.3.7.

### Novello, Clara, 1818–1908.

**4.4.14**   A.L.s. to Elizabeth Montgomery
Severn; [London], 1 June 1852.

3p. on 2 conjugate leaves, 10.8 x 8.8 cm. Laid
paper with fragment of unidentified
watermark; embossed with initials C G.

Same provenance as 4.3.7.

**4.4.15**   A.L.s. to Joseph Severn; [n.p.],
7 June 1875.

3p. on 2 conjugate leaves, 10.4 x 13.2 cm. Laid
paper unwatermarked.

Same provenance as 4.3.7.

### Novello, Vincent, 1781–1861.

**4.4.16**   A.L.s. to Joseph Severn;
[London], 22 October 1842.

4p. on 2 conjugate leaves, 18.7 x 11.5 cm.
Wove paper unwatermarked.

Same provenance as 4.3.7.

**4.4.17**   A.L.s. to Joseph Severn;
[London], 25 November 1843.

2p. on 1 leaf, 22.8 x 18.7 cm. Wove paper
unwatermarked.

Same provenance as 4.3.7.

### Clarke, Charles Cowden, 1787–1877.

**4.4.18**   A few memoranda of the early life of
John Keats.

A.MS. (unsigned); [London, 16 March 1846].
*KC* 187.

12p. on 12 leaves, 28.2 x 22.5 cm. Wove paper
unwatermarked.

Once accompanied 4.4.2.

Same provenance as 1.14. Presented by Arthur A.
Houghton, Jr., 1970.

**4.4.19**   Recollections of John Keats.

A.MS.s.; [n.p., 1860?]. *KC* 264 (in part).

68p. on 63 leaves, 23.2 x 14.3 cm. Wove paper
unwatermarked.

Presented by Arthur A. Houghton, Jr., 1970.

Substantially as printed in Charles and Mary Cowden
Clarke, *Recollections of Writers* (1878), 120-157.

### Dilke, Charles Wentworth, 1789–1864.

**4.5.1**   A.L.s. to George Keats;
[London], 12 February 1833. *KC* 150.

4p. on 2 conjugate leaves, 22.3 x 18.3 cm. Laid
paper watermarked with triple plume flanked
by script G D, with date 1831. Silked.

Purchased from John Wilson Townsend, Louisville,
Kentucky, through gifts of Friends of the Library, 1943.

**4.5.2**    A.L.s. to George Keats; [London], September [1838]. *KC* 157.

4p. on 2 conjugate leaves, 18.6 x 11.5 cm. Wove paper unwatermarked.

Same provenance as 4.5.1.

**4.5.3**    A.L.s. to Joseph Severn; [London, April[?] 1841]. *KC* 170.

6p. on 2 pairs of conjugate leaves, 18.3 x 11.7 cm. Wove paper unwatermarked.

Same provenance as 1.14. Presented by Arthur A. Houghton, Jr., 1970.

**4.5.4**    A.L.s. to [Richard Monckton Milnes, Baron Houghton]; [London], 3 September [1846?]. *KC* 195.

4p. on 2 conjugate leaves, 18 x 11.2 cm. Wove paper unwatermarked.

Same provenance as 1.14. Presented by Arthur A. Houghton, Jr., 1970.

**4.5.5**    A.L.s. to Richard Monckton Milnes, Baron Houghton; [London], 28 December [1846]. *KC* 206.

6p. on 2 pairs of conjugate leaves, 18.2 x 11.2 cm. Wove paper unwatermarked.

Same provenance as 1.14. Presented by Arthur A. Houghton, Jr., 1970.

**4.5.6**    A.L.s. to [Richard Monckton Milnes, Baron Houghton]; Bedhampton, 2 June [1847?]. *KC* 228.

3p. on 2 conjugate leaves, 18.4 x 11 cm. Wove paper unwatermarked.

Same provenance as 1.14. Presented by Arthur A. Houghton, Jr., 1970.

**4.5.7**    A.L.s. to [Richard Monckton Milnes, Baron Houghton]; [London, ca. 15 August 1848]. *KC* 243.

4p. on 2 conjugate leaves, 18 x 11.2 cm. Wove paper unwatermarked.

Same provenance as 1.14. Presented by Arthur A. Houghton, Jr., 1970.

**4.5.8**    A.L.s. to Richard Monckton Milnes, Baron Houghton; [London, January 1875?]. *KC* 277.

1p. on 2 conjugate leaves of mourning paper, 11.6 x 9.1 cm. Laid paper watermarked: Joy[NER] | I[8  ].

Same provenance as 1.14. Presented by Arthur A. Houghton, Jr., 1970.

**4.5.9**    A.L.s. to Richard Monckton Milnes, Baron Houghton; [London], 6 February 1875. *KC* 278.

1p. on 2 conjugate leaves of mourning paper, 17.7 x 11.5 cm. Laid paper watermarked: [script] I & I A  | [roman] KENT.

Same provenance as 1.14. Presented by Arthur A. Houghton, Jr., 1970.

**4.5.10**    Notes on Lord Houghton's life of John Keats.

A.MS. (unsigned, fragmentary); [London, January 1875?]. *KC* 276.

1p. on 1 leaf, 32 x 20 cm., laid paper watermarked: J ALLEN & SONS | SUPERFINE | 1872; and 2p. on 2 leaves, 17.7 x 11.4 cm., same paper as 4.5.9.

Same provenance as 1.14. Presented by Arthur A. Houghton, Jr., 1970.

**4.5.11**    Dilke, Charles Wentworth, transcriber. John Keats. MS.L. (transcript) to Mrs. Samuel Brawne; Naples Harbour, 24 October [1820]. Rollins 305.

2p. on 2 leaves, 32 x 20 cm. Same paper as folio sheet in 4.5.10.

Same provenance as 1.14. Presented by Arthur A. Houghton, Jr., 1970.

*Dilke, William, 1796–1885.*

**4.5.12**    A.L.s. (initials) to Charles Wentworth Dilke; [n.p.], 15 February [1875?]. *KC 279.*

2p. on 1 leaf, 11.5 x 8.7 cm. Laid paper unwatermarked.

Same provenance as 1.14. Presented by Arthur A. Houghton, Jr., 1970.

*Haslam, William, 1795?–1851.*

**4.6.1**    A.L. (3d person) to John Taylor; [London, 13 September 1820]. *KC 63.*

2p. on 2 conjugate leaves, 23 x 18.5 cm. Laid paper watermarked with crowned posthorn.

Presented by Lucius Wilmerding, 1946.

**4.6.2**    A.L.s. to Taylor & Hessey; [London], 23 September 1820. *KC 71.*

2p. on 2 conjugate leaves, 22.9 x 18.6 cm. Laid paper watermarked: GILLING & ALLFORD 1816.

Same provenance as 4.6.1.

**4.6.3**    A.L.s. to Joseph Severn; Greenwich, 4 December 1820.

4p. on 2 conjugate leaves, 25.7 x 20.4 cm. Laid paper watermarked with crowned posthorn and script G R M.

Same provenance as 4.3.7.

**4.6.4**    A.L.s. to [Richard Monckton Milnes, Baron Houghton]; [London], 5 February 1847. *KC 213.*

2p. on 2 conjugate leaves, 25.2 x 20 cm. Blue wove paper unwatermarked.

Same provenance as 1.14. Presented by Arthur A. Houghton, Jr., 1970.

**4.6.5**    A.L.s. to Richard Monckton Milnes, Baron Houghton; [London], 8 May 1847. *KC 223.*

3p. on 2 conjugate leaves, 25.2 x 20 cm. Same paper as 4.6.4.

Same provenance as 1.14. Presented by Arthur A. Houghton, Jr., 1970.

**4.6.6**    A.L. (unsigned draft) to [Richard Monckton Milnes, Baron Houghton]; [London], 19 August 1848. *KC 244.*

3p. on 2 conjugate leaves, 25.2 x 20.5 cm. Blue wove paper unwatermarked.

Same provenance as 1.14. Presented by Arthur A. Houghton, Jr., 1970.

**4.6.7**    A.L.s. (initials) to Richard Monckton Milnes, Baron Houghton; [London], 23 August 1848. *KC 247.*

1p. on 1 leaf, 25.2 x 20.2 cm. Blue wove paper unwatermarked.

Same provenance as 1.14. Presented by Arthur A. Houghton, Jr., 1970.

*Haydon, Benjamin Robert, 1786–1846.*

**4.7.1**    A.L. (unsigned, in verse) to [John Hamilton Reynolds]; [London, October 1816]. *KC 2.*

2p. on 1 leaf, 23 x 19 cm. Laid paper watermarked: PHIPPS & SONS.

Presented by Arthur A. Houghton, Jr., 1970.

**4.7.2**    A.L.s. to John Keats; [London], 3 March 1817. Rollins 15.

2p. on 1 leaf, 23.8 x 18.5 cm. Laid paper, fragment of watermark: [script] P & S.

Formerly attached to Haydon's manuscript journal.

Presented by Arthur A. Houghton, Jr., 1952.

**4.7.3**    A.L.s. to John Keats; [London], March 1817. Rollins 17.

4p. on 2 conjugate leaves, 27.8 x 18.9 cm. Laid paper watermarked: PHIPPS & SONS | 1816.

Same provenance as 4.7.2.

**4.7.4**   A.L.s. to John Keats;
[London, 8? May 1817]. Rollins 23.

4p. on 2 conjugate leaves, 33.5 x 20 cm. Laid
paper watermarked: J Snelgrove | 1815, with
countermark of seated Britannia in an oval.
Portion of second leaf torn away.

Same provenance as 4.7.2.

**4.7.5**   A.L.s. to John Keats;
[London], 8 May 1817. Rollins 24.

1p. on 1 leaf, 22 x 18 cm. Laid paper with
fragment of watermark: [script] T I C.

Same provenance as 4.7.2.

**4.7.6**   A.L.s. to John Keats;
[London], 17 September 1817. Rollins 35.

2p. on 1 leaf, 25.3 x 20.3 cm. Same paper as 4.7.5.

Same provenance as 4.7.2.

**4.7.7**   A.L. (fragment, wanting end) to John
Keats; [London, 11 January 1818]. Rollins 51.

2p. on 1 leaf, 22.2 x 18.3 cm. Same paper as 4.7.5.

Same provenance as 4.7.2.

**4.7.8**   A.L.s. to John Keats;
[London], 4 March 1818. Rollins 66.

1p. on 1 leaf, 22.3 x 18 cm. Same paper as 4.7.5.

Same provenance as 4.7.2.

**4.7.9**   A.L.s. to John Keats;
[London], 25 March 1818. Rollins 73.

4p. on 2 conjugate leaves, 22.3 x 18 cm. Same
paper as 4.7.5.

Same provenance as 4.7.2.

**4.7.10**   MS.L.s., with A. postscript, to John
Keats; Bridgewater, 25 September [1818].
Rollins 109.

4p. on 2 leaves, 22.7 x 18.4 cm. Wove paper
watermarked: [script] G S | 1812.

William Harris Arnold; E. S. Burgess. Presented by
Arthur A. Houghton, Jr., 1970.

**4.7.11**   A.L.s. to John Keats;
[London, 23[?] December 1818]. Rollins 132.

4p. on 2 conjugate leaves, 22.7 x 18.3 cm. Wove
paper watermarked with crowned posthorn
and unidentified monogram. Right edge
damaged, affecting text.

Same provenance as 4.7.2.

**4.7.12**   A.L.s. to John Keats;
[London, 1 January 1819?]. Rollins 136.

1p. on 1 leaf, 23.7 x 18.7 cm. Laid paper
watermarked: Phipps & Sons.

Same provenance as 4.7.2.

**4.7.13**   A.L.s. to John Keats;
[London], 7 January 1819. Rollins 139.

1p. on 1 leaf, 22.8 x 18.2 cm. Same paper as
4.7.11.

Same provenance as 4.7.2.

**4.7.14**   A.L.s. to John Keats;
[London], 14 January 1819. Rollins 141.

1p. on 1 leaf, 19.7 x 12.2 cm. Laid paper,
fragment of watermark: 18[   ].

Same provenance as 4.7.2.

**4.7.15**   A.L.s. to John Keats;
[London], 21 [i.e. 20] February 1819. Rollins 147.

2p. on 1 leaf, 22.7 x 18 cm. Same paper as 4.7.11.

Same provenance as 4.7.2.

**4.7.16**   A.L.s. to John Keats;
[London], 10 March [1819]. Rollins 150.

4p. on 2 conjugate leaves, 19.6 x 12.5 cm. Laid
paper, fragment of watermark: [script] J B.

Same provenance as 4.7.2.

**4.7.17**   A.L.s. to John Keats;
[London, 12 April 1819]. Rollins 156.

3p. on 2 conjugate leaves, 19.8 x 15.7 cm. Laid
paper watermarked: 1816.

Same provenance as 4.7.2.

**4.7.18** A.L.s. to John Keats; [London, June 1820]. Rollins 265.

2p. on 1 leaf, 22.6 x 18.5 cm. Wove paper watermarked with triple plume and script J & M | 1818.

Same provenance as 4.7.2.

**4.7.19** A.L.s. to John Keats; [London], 14 July 1820. Rollins 274.

3p. on 2 conjugate leaves, 22.9 x 18.6 cm. Laid paper watermarked with crowned posthorn and script J R A.

Same provenance as 4.7.2.

**4.7.20** A.L.s. to Edward Moxon; London, 28 November 1845. Contains transcripts of: *Haydon! forgive me that I cannot speak* and *My spirit is too weak—mortality. KC* 184.

4p. on 2 conjugate leaves, 23.3 x 18.8 cm. Wove paper unwatermarked.

Presented by Arthur A. Houghton, Jr., 1970.

**4.7.21** A.L.s. to [Edward Moxon]; London, 29 November 1845. *KC* 185.

7p. on 2 pairs of conjugate leaves, 19 x 11.6 cm. Wove paper unwatermarked.

Bequeathed by Amy Lowell, 1925.

**4.7.22** A.L.s. to Edward Moxon; London, 30 November 1845. *KC* 186.

3p. on 2 conjugate leaves, 18.8 x 11.8 cm. Wove paper unwatermarked.

Presented by Arthur A. Houghton, Jr., 1970.

**4.7.23** A.L. (3d person) to [Richard Monckton Milnes]; London, 28 May 1846. *KC* 193.

2p. on 2 conjugate leaves, 18.4 x 11.6 cm. Wove paper unwatermarked. A. note by Milnes on p.2.

Same provenance as 1.14. Presented by Arthur A. Houghton, Jr., 1970.

**4.7.24** Transcripts of letters and parts of letters from John Keats to Benjamin Robert Haydon and Tom Keats.

MS. in Haydon's hand; [London, 1845-1846].

2p. on 1 leaf, 32 x 20.2 cm. Blue wove paper unwatermarked. 6p. on 6 leaves, 22.5 x 18.5 cm. Wove paper watermarked with triple plume and script J M & M. 2p. on 1 leaf, 23.2 x 18.8 cm. Bluish wove paper unwatermarked.

Contains all or parts of the following letters: Rollins 11, 12, 26, 37, 97, 140, 149, and 289.

Same provenance as 1.14. Presented by Arthur A. Houghton, Jr., 1970.

### Hessey, J. A. (James Augustus), 1785–1870.

*see also 4.19.1-.10*

**4.8.1** A.L.s. to John Taylor; Kinsale, 19 August 1806. *KC* 301.

4p. on 2 conjugate leaves, 22.3 x 18.2 cm. Wove paper watermarked: B S | 1805.

Presented by Lucius Wilmerding, 1946.

**4.8.2** A.L.s. to John Taylor; [London], 2 June 1809. *KC* 302.

4p. on 2 conjugate leaves, 23 x 18.7 cm. Laid paper watermarked with crowned posthorn and initials G R.

Same provenance as 4.8.1.

**4.8.3** A.L.s. to John Taylor; London, 4 October 1809. *KC* 303.

4p. on 2 conjugate leaves, 22.8 x 18.5 cm. Wove paper unwatermarked.

Same provenance as 4.8.1.

**4.8.4** A.L.s. to John Taylor; London, 9 May 1810. *KC* 304.

4p. on 2 conjugate leaves, 22.7 x 18.4 cm. Wove paper watermarked: Ruse & Turners | 1807.

Same provenance as 4.8.1.

**4.8.5**   A.L.s. to John Taylor;
[London], 31 July 1810. *KC* 305.

4p. on 2 conjugate leaves, 29.8 x 18.6 cm. Wove
paper watermarked: 1804.

Same provenance as 4.8.1.

**4.8.6**   A.L.s. to John Taylor;
Bath, 12 October 1810. *KC* 306.

4p. on 2 conjugate leaves, 22.3 x 18.3 cm. Laid
paper watermarked: Edmeads & Pine.

Same provenance as 4.8.1.

**4.8.7**   A.L.s. to John Taylor;
[London], 10 May 1811. *KC* 307.

4p. on 2 conjugate leaves, 22.7 x 18.6 cm. Laid
paper watermarked with crowned posthorn.

Same provenance as 4.8.1.

**4.8.8**   A.L.s. to John Taylor;
[London], 14 June 1811. *KC* 308.

4p. on 2 conjugate leaves, 22.5 x 18.5 cm. Wove
paper watermarked: L Tovil Mill | 1810.

Same provenance as 4.8.1.

**4.8.9**   A.L.s. to John Taylor;
[London], 24 June 1811. *KC* 309.

4p. on 2 conjugate leaves, 22.5 x 18.5 cm. Same
paper as 4.8.8.

Same provenance as 4.8.1.

**4.8.10**   A.L.s. to John Taylor;
[London], 2 July 1811. *KC* 310.

4p. on 2 conjugate leaves, 22.7 x 18.5 cm. Same
paper as 4.8.7.

Same provenance as 4.8.1.

**4.8.11**   A.L.s. to John Taylor;
[London], 19 October 1813. *KC* 311.

2p. on 2 conjugate leaves, 22.9 x 18.5 cm. Wove
paper watermarked: Bath | 1812.

Same provenance as 4.8.1.

**4.8.12**   A.L.s. to John Taylor;
[London], 17 December 1813. *KC* 312.

4p. on 2 conjugate leaves, 22.9 x 18.6 cm. Same
paper as 4.8.11.

Same provenance as 4.8.1.

**4.8.13**   A.L.s. to John Taylor;
London, 21 December 1813. *KC* 313.

4p. on 2 conjugate leaves, 22.9 x 18.7 cm. Same
paper as 4.8.11.

Same provenance as 4.8.1.

**4.8.14**   A.L.s. to John Taylor;
[London], 12 August 1814. *KC* 314.

4p. on 2 conjugate leaves, 23 x 18.5 cm. Wove
paper watermarked: T Stains | 1813.

Same provenance as 4.8.1.

**4.8.15**   A.L.s. to John Taylor;
[London], 22 July 1815. *KC* 315.

4p. on 2 conjugate leaves, 23.4 x 18.9 cm. Wove
paper unwatermarked.

Same provenance as 4.8.1.

**4.8.16**   A.L.s. to John Taylor;
London, 31 July 1815. *KC* 316.

4p. on 2 conjugate leaves, 23.2 x 19 cm. Wove
paper unwatermarked.

Same provenance as 4.8.1.

**4.8.17**   A.L.s. to John Taylor;
[London], 29 August 1817. *KC* 317.

4p. on 2 conjugate leaves, 32.6 x 20.3 cm. Wove
paper watermarked: I I Smith & Co | 1817.

Same provenance as 4.8.1.

**4.8.18**   A.L.s. to John Taylor;
[London], 5 September 1818. *KC* 16.

2p. on 1 leaf, 32.7 x 20.1 cm. Same paper as
4.8.17.

Same provenance as 4.8.1.

**4.8.19**   A.L.s. to John Taylor;
London, 23 October 1818. *KC* 22.

4p. on 2 conjugate leaves, 23 x 18.5 cm. Wove
paper unwatermarked.

Same provenance as 4.8.1.

**4.8.20**   A.L.s. to John Taylor;
London, 7 October 1822. *KC* 318.

4p. on 2 conjugate leaves, 22.7 x 18.8 cm. Laid
paper watermarked with crowned posthorn
and unidentified monogram.

Same provenance as 4.8.1.

**4.8.21**   A.L.s. to John Taylor;
[London], 5 November 1822. *KC* 319.

4p. on 2 conjugate leaves, 22.6 x 18.3 cm. Wove
paper watermarked: BASTED MILL | 1820.

Same provenance as 4.8.1.

4.8.22   A.L.s. to John Taylor;
[London], 15 January 1823. *KC* 320.

4p. on 2 conjugate leaves, 22.7 x 18.8 cm. Same
paper as 4.8.21.

Same provenance as 4.8.1.

**4.8.23**   A.L.s. to John Taylor;
London, 21–22 January 1823. *KC* 324.

4p. on 2 conjugate leaves, 22.7 x 18.6 cm. Same
paper as 4.8.21.

Same provenance as 4.8.1.

**4.8.24**   A.L.s. to John Taylor;
[London], 14 March 1825. *KC* 325.

4p. on 2 conjugate leaves, 22.5 x 18.2 cm. Wove
paper watermarked: J WHATMAN | 1821.

Same provenance as 4.8.1.

**4.8.25**   A.L.s. to John Taylor;
[London, 17 March 1823]. *KC* 326.

4p. on 2 conjugate leaves, 23 x 18.7 cm. Wove
paper unwatermarked.

Same provenance as 4.8.1.

**4.8.26**   A.L.s. to John Taylor;
[London], 18 March [1823]. *KC* 327.

4p. on 2 conjugate leaves, 22.3 x 18.3 cm. Laid
paper watermarked: J WHATMAN | 1818.

Same provenance as 4.8.1.

**4.8.27**   A.L.s. to John Taylor;
[London], 21 March 1823. *KC* 328.

4p. on 2 conjugate leaves, 23 x 18.8 cm. Wove
paper unwatermarked.

Same provenance as 4.8.1.

**4.8.28**   A.L.s. to John Taylor;
[London], 21 [March 1823]. *KC* 329.

3p. on 2 conjugate leaves, 22.5 x 18.2 cm. Wove
paper unwatermarked.

Same provenance as 4.8.1.

**4.8.29**   A.L.s. to John Taylor;
[London, ca. 25 March 1823]. *KC* 330.

2p. on 2 conjugate leaves, 18.7 x 11.3 cm. Laid
paper watermarked with posthorn and script J
& E G.

Same provenance as 4.8.1.

**4.8.30**   A.L.s. to John Taylor;
[London, 26 March 1824]. *KC* 331.

2p. on 1 leaf, 22.3 x 18.4 cm. Same paper as
4.8.20.

Same provenance as 4.8.1.

**4.8.31**   A.L.s. to John Taylor;
[London, 27 March 1823]. *KC* 332.

1p. on 1 leaf, 22.5 x 18.4 cm. Same paper as
4.8.20.

Same provenance as 4.8.1.

**4.8.32**   A.L.s. to John Taylor;
[London], 23 April 1823. *KC* 333.

2p. on 1 leaf, 22.6 x 18.3 cm. Laid paper
watermarked: GATER.

Same provenance as 4.8.1.

**4.8.33**   A.L.s. to John Taylor;
[London], 1 July [1823]. *KC* 334.

2p. on 1 leaf, 18.4 x 11.4 cm. Same paper as
4.8.21.

Same provenance as 4.8.1.

**4.8.34**   A.L.s. to John Taylor;
[London], 3 September [1823]. *KC* 336.

4p. on 2 conjugate leaves, 18.5 x 11.4 cm. Same
paper as 4.8.21.

Same provenance as 4.8.1.

**4.8.35**   A.L.s. to John Taylor;
[London], 23 September 1823. *KC* 337.

4p. on 2 conjugate leaves, 22.9 x 18.5 cm. Same
paper as 4.8.21.

Same provenance as 4.8.1.

**4.8.36**   A.L.s. to John Taylor;
[London], 20 October 1823. *KC* 338.

4p. on 2 conjugate leaves, 20.4 x 12.4 cm. Wove
paper unwatermarked.

Same provenance as 4.8.1.

**4.8.37**   A.L.s. to John Taylor;
[London], 30 June 1826. *KC* 344.

4p. on 2 conjugate leaves, 18.7 x 11.4 cm. Wove
paper watermarked: BASTED MILL | 1824.

**4.8.38**   A.L.s. to John Taylor;
Bournemouth, 20 December 1853. *KC* 261.

4p. on 2 conjugate leaves, 18 x 11.1 cm. Laid
paper watermarked: [B?]USBRIDGE.

Same provenance as 4.8.1.

**4.8.39**   A.L.s. to John Taylor;
Brightstone, 16 June 1858. *KC* 349.

4p. on 2 conjugate leaves of mourning paper,
17.5 x 11.3 cm. Laid paper watermarked:
JOYNSON | 1857.

Same provenance as 4.8.1.

**4.8.40**   A.L.s. to John Taylor;
Manningford, 15 August 1860. *KC* 350.

4p. on 2 conjugate leaves of mourning paper, 18
x 11.4 cm. Laid paper watermarked: JOYNSON |
1860.

Same provenance as 4.8.1.

### Hunt, Leigh, 1784–1859.

**4.9.1**   A.L.s. to Joseph Severn;
Genoa, 10 May 1823.

3p. on 2 conjugate leaves, 25 x 19.2 cm. Wove
paper watermarked: G A | P.

Same provenance as 4.3.7.

**4.9.2**   A.L.s. to Richard Monckton Milnes,
Baron Houghton; [London], 7 May [1846].
*KC* 191.

2p. on 2 conjugate leaves, 11.1 x 9.1 cm. Wove
paper watermarked: J WHA[TMAN] | 18[46?]
(same as 4.9.3?)

Same provenance as 1.14. Presented by Arthur A.
Houghton, Jr., 1970.

**4.9.3**   Transcript of *Who loves to peer up at the
morning sun.*

MS. in Leigh Hunt's hand; [London, 1846?].

1p. on 1 leaf, 22.3 x 18.2 cm. Wove paper
watermarked: J WHATMAN | 1846.

Same provenance as 1.14. Presented by Arthur A.
Houghton, Jr., 1970.

**4.9.4**   A.L.s. to Richard Monckton Milnes,
Baron Houghton; [London],
22 December [1846]. *KC* 203.

4p. on 2 conjugate leaves, 11.1 x 8.9 cm. Wove
paper unwatermarked.

Same provenance as 1.14. Presented by Arthur A.
Houghton, Jr., 1970.

**4.9.5**  A.L.s. to Richard Monckton Milnes, Baron Houghton; [London], 21 January [1847]. *KC* 210.

4p. on 2 conjugate leaves, 11.1 x 9 cm. Laid paper with fragment of unidentified watermark.

Same provenance as 1.14. Presented by Arthur A. Houghton, Jr., 1970.

### Keats, George, 1797–1842.

**4.10.1**  A.L.s. to Marian and Sarah Jeffrey; Hampstead, [March 1818]. *KC* 6.

4p. on 2 conjugate leaves, 22.2 x 18.3 cm. Wove paper watermarked: IVY MILL | 1816. Silked.

Same provenance as 4.7.10. Presented by Arthur A. Houghton, Jr., 1970.

**4.10.2**  A.L.s. to John Keats; [London], 18 March 1818. Rollins 69.

4p. on 2 conjugate leaves, 24.8 x 19.9 cm. Laid paper watermarked with crowned posthorn and script Y & M.

Bequeathed by Amy Lowell, 1925.

**4.10.3**  A.L.s. to John Taylor; [London, ca. 18 June 1818]. *KC* 12. Rollins 87.

4p. on 2 conjugate leaves, 23.4 x 18.8 cm. Wove paper watermarked: RUSE & TURNERS | 1817.

Bequeathed by Amy Lowell, 1925.

**4.10.4**  A.L.s. to Fanny Keats; Louisville, 25 May 1820–6 January 1821. *KC* 50.

2p. on 1 leaf, 25.4 x 20.1 cm. Wove paper watermarked: M.

Same provenance as 4.7.10. Presented by Arthur A. Houghton, Jr., 1970.

**4.10.5**  A.L.s. to John Keats; Louisville, 18 June 1820. Rollins 264.

2p. on 1 leaf, 25.4 x 20.1 cm. Same paper as 4.9.10.

Bequeathed by Amy Lowell, 1925.

**4.10.6**  A.L.s. to John Keats; Louisville, 8 November 1820. Rollins 308.

2p. on 1 leaf, 24.7 x 19.9 cm. Wove paper unwatermarked.

Bequeathed by Amy Lowell, 1925.

**4.10.7**  A.L.s. to [Charles Armitage Brown]; Louisville, 3 March 1821. *KC* 106.

1p. on 1 leaf, 21.8 x 19.8 cm. Wove paper unwatermarked.

Bequeathed by Amy Lowell, 1925.

**4.10.8**  A.L.s. to Charles Wentworth Dilke; Louisville, 10 April 1824. *KC* 133.

4p. on 2 conjugate leaves, 31.8 x 19.6 cm. Wove paper unwatermarked.

Bequeathed by Amy Lowell, 1925.

**4.10.9**  A.L.s. to Charles Wentworth Dilke; Louisville, 20 April 1825. *KC* 136.

6p. on 1 leaf and 1 pair of conjugate leaves, 31.1 x 19.7 cm. Wove paper unwatermarked.

Bequeathed by Amy Lowell, 1925.

**4.10.10**  A.L.s. to [Charles Wentworth Dilke]; Louisville, 18 October 1826. *KC* 139.

2p. on 1 leaf, 24.8 x 20 cm. Wove paper watermarked: OWEN & HURLBURT.

Bequeathed by Amy Lowell, 1925.

**4.10.11**  A.L.s. to Charles Wentworth Dilke; Louisville, 25 March 1828. *KC* 141.

4p. on 2 conjugate leaves, 25.1 x 20.7 cm. Wove paper watermarked: HUDSON.

Bequeathed by Amy Lowell, 1925.

**4.10.12**  A.L.s. to Charles Wentworth Dilke; Louisville, 16 April–New York, 12 May 1828. *KC* 142.

4p. on 2 conjugate leaves, 25.2 x 20 cm. Wove paper unwatermarked.

Bequeathed by Amy Lowell, 1925.

**4.10.13**   A.L.s. to Charles Wentworth Dilke;
Louisville, 12 July 1828. *KC* 143.

3p. on 2 conjugate leaves, 25.2 x 20.7 cm. Same
paper as 4.10.11.

Bequeathed by Amy Lowell, 1925.

**4.10.14**   A.L.s. to Maria Dilke;
Louisville, 19 March 1829. *KC* 145.

4p. on 2 conjugate leaves, 25.1 x 20 cm. Wove
paper watermarked: AMIES | PHILAD^A.

Bequeathed by Amy Lowell, 1925.

**4.10.15**   A.L.s. to Charles Wentworth Dilke;
Louisville, 14 November 1829. *KC* 146.

4p. on 2 conjugate leaves, 25.8 x 20 cm. Laid
paper watermarked: AMIES | PHILAD^A, with
countermark of a bird.

Bequeathed by Amy Lowell, 1925.

**4.10.16**   A.L.s. to Charles Wentworth Dilke;
Louisville, 7 May 1830. *KC* 147.

4p. on 2 conjugate leaves, 31.8 x 19.8 cm. Wove
paper unwatermarked.

Bequeathed by Amy Lowell, 1925.

**4.10.17**   A.L.s. to Charles Wentworth Dilke;
Louisville, 22 November 1830. *KC* 148.

2p. on 1 leaf, 25 x 20 cm. Laid paper
unwatermarked.

Bequeathed by Amy Lowell, 1925.

**4.10.18**   A.L.s. to Charles Wentworth Dilke;
Louisville, 11 May 1832. *KC* 149.

4p. on 2 conjugate leaves, 25.2 x 21 cm. Bluish
wove paper, watermarked: B P & C.

Bequeathed by Amy Lowell, 1925.

**4.10.19**   A.L.s. to Charles Wentworth Dilke;
Louisville 23 [i.e. 24] November–14 December
1833. *KC* 151.

4p. on 2 conjugate leaves, 31 x 18.6 cm. Wove
paper unwatermarked.

Bequeathed by Amy Lowell, 1925.

**4.10.20**   A.L.s. to Charles Wentworth Dilke;
Louisville, 14 March–8 October 1836. *KC* 153.

4p. on 2 conjugate leaves, 25.3 x 19.8 cm. Wove
paper watermarked with parallel lines and:
J. ROBINSON | PHIL^A.

Bequeathed by Amy Lowell, 1925.

**4.10.21**   A.L.s. to Lewis Jacob Cist;
Louisville, 18 June 1837. *KC* 155.

2p. on 2 conjugate leaves, 23.1 x 18.7. Same
paper as 4.10.20.

Lewis Jacob Cist (sale, 1886, lot 2856); John A. Spoor
(sale, 27 April 1939, part of lot 463). Presented by
Arthur A. Houghton, Jr., 1970.

**4.10.22**   A.L.s. to Charles Wentworth Dilke;
Louisville, 1 March 1838. *KC* 156.

4p. on 2 conjugate leaves, 25.2 x 19.9 cm. Same
paper as 4.10.20.

Bequeathed by Amy Lowell, 1925.

**4.10.23**   A.L.s. to J. F. Clarke;
Louisville, 10 August 1839. *KC* 158.

2p. on 2 conjugate leaves, 25.3 x 20.2 cm. Bluish
wove paper, ruled, watermarked: O & H.

Presented by J. F. Clarke, 1946.

**4.10.24**   A.L.s. to Anna H. Barker Ward;
Louisville, 15 November 1839. *KC* 159.

2p. on 2 conjugate leaves, 25 x 19.6 cm. White
wove paper, ruled, watermarked: AMIES |
PHIL^A.

Same provenance as 2.27, which it formerly accom-
panied.

**4.10.25**   A.L.s. to J. F. Clarke;
Louisville, 25 November 1840. *KC* 162.

4p. on 2 conjugate leaves, 25.2 x 20.3 cm. Bluish
laid paper, ruled, watermarked: O & H.

Same provenance as 4.10.23.

**4.10.26** A.L.s. to J. F. Clarke; Louisville, 17 January 1841. *KC* 163.

4p. on 2 conjugate leaves, 25.3 x 20.3 cm. Same paper as 4.10.25.

Same provenance as 4.10.23.

**4.10.27** A.L.s. to J. F. Clarke; Louisville, 4 July 1841. *KC* 171.

4p. on 2 conjugate leaves, 25.4 x 20.3 cm. Same paper as 4.10.25.

Same provenance as 4.10.23.

### Keats, Georgiana Augusta Wylie, 1802?–1879.

**4.10.28** A.L.s. to [Alexander Jeffrey]; [Louisville, n.d.].

4p. on 2 conjugate leaves, 25.2 x 19.8 cm. Wove paper unwatermarked.

Purchased through gifts of Friends of the Library, 1943.

**4.10.29** A.L.s. to Lewis Jacob Cist; Louisville, 2 April 1844.

2p. on 2 conjugate leaves, 25.2 x 20.3 cm. Same paper as 4.10.25.

Presented by Arthur A. Houghton, Jr., 1970.

### Keats, John Henry, 1827–1917.

**4.10.30** A.L.s. to Dewitt Miller; Maysville, 11 March 1895.

1p. on 1 leaf, 21.8 x 14.1 cm.

Purchased with the Edgar H. Wells Fund, 1941.

**4.10.31** A.L.s. to Dewitt Miller; Maysville, 15 August 1895.

1p. on 1 leaf, 21.3 x 15.3 cm.

Same provenance as 4.10.30.

**4.10.32** A.L.s. to Dewitt Miller; Maysville, 19 March 1900.

2p. on 2 leaves, 21.7 x 14.1 cm.

Same provenance as 4.10.30.

**4.10.33** MS.L. (dictated to Juanita Keats) to Dewitt Miller; Maysville, 22 February 1909.

2p. on 2 conjugate leaves, 16.5 x 13 cm.

Same provenance as 4.10.30.

### Keats, Tom, 1799–1818.

**4.11.1** A.L.s. to Marian Jeffrey; Hampstead, [1] May 1818. *KC* 9. Rollins 82.

4p. on 2 conjugate leaves, 22.6 x 18.6 cm. Wove paper watermarked: JOHN HAYES | 1817.

Albert Forbes Sieveking (embossed stamp); Frank B. Bemis. Presented by Arthur A. Houghton, Jr., 1970.

**4.11.2** A.L.s. to John Taylor; Hampstead, 22 June 1818. *KC* 13. Rollins 90.

2p. on 1 leaf, 24.2 x 19.1 cm. Laid paper watermarked with crowned fleur-de-lys.

Bequeathed by Amy Lowell, 1925.

**4.11.3** A.L.s. to John Taylor; Hampstead, [30 June 1818]. *KC* 14.

2p. on 2 conjugate leaves, 23.2 x 18.8 cm. Wove paper unwatermarked.

Bequeathed by Amy Lowell, 1925.

### Keats, Fanny, 1803–1889.

**4.12.1** A.L.s. to George Keats; [London], 31 May 1826. *KC* 138.

Includes a short autograph note by Valentin Llanos, and Fanny's transcript of Shelley's *Adonais*, omitting stanzas 19-24.

4p. on 2 conjugate leaves, 22.7 x 18.7 cm. Wove paper watermarked: GREEN & SON | 1825. Silked; a photostatic copy made before silking is on file.

Purchased with gifts of Friends of the Library, 1943.

**4.12.2**    A.L.s. to Joseph Severn;
Madrid, 3 September 1877.

3p. on 2 conjugate leaves, 21.1 x 13.2 cm. Wove
paper unwatermarked, ruled.

Presented by Arthur A. Houghton, Jr., 1954.

**4.12.3**    Speed, John Gilmer, 1853-1909. A.L.s. to
Fanny Keats; New York, 29 July 1877.

4p. on 2 conjugate leaves, 20.2 x 13.1 cm. Laid
paper watermarked: [all gothic] 1776 1876 |
Centennial | T R P | Co.

Same provenance as 4.12.2.

**4.12.4**    MS.L.s. to [F. Holland Day];
Madrid, 26 September 1889.

2p. on 2 conjugate leaves of mourning paper,
20.1 x 12.5 cm.; with envelope. Laid paper,
ruled, watermarked: TOWGOOD'S | EXTRA
SUPER.

Purchased with the Henry Saltonstall Howe Fund,
1934.

**4.12.5**    MS.L. to F. Holland Day;
Madrid, 30 October [1889].

2p. on 2 conjugate leaves, 20.1 x 12.5 cm.; with
envelope. Same paper as 4.12.4.

Same provenance as 4.12.4.

**4.12.6**    MS.L. to F. Holland Day;
Madrid, 12 November 1889.

3p. on 2 conjugate leaves, 20.1 x 12.5 cm.; with
envelope. Same paper as 4.12.4.

Same provenance as 4.12.4.

**4.12.7**    Forman, H. Buxton (Harry Buxton),
1842-1917. MS.L. (transcript by Rosa Llanos y
Keats) to [Fanny Keats]; [n.p.], 14 February
1890.

Same provenance as 4.12.4.

*Llanos y Keats, Rosa, 1833–1905.*

**4.12.8**    A.L.s. to F. Holland Day;
Madrid, 30 March 1890.

6p. on 2 pairs of conjugate leaves of mourning
paper, 17.6 x 11.4 cm.; with envelope. Laid
paper watermarked with crown and: [gothic]
Abbey Mills | Greenfield.

Same provenance as 4.12.4.

**4.12.9**    A.L.s. to F. Holland Day;
Madrid, 20 May 1890.

4p. on 2 conjugate leaves, 17.6 x 11.4 cm.; with
envelope. Same paper as 4.12.8.

Same provenance as 4.12.4.

**4.12.10**    A.L.s. to F. Holland Day;
Madrid, 31 August 1890.

3p. on 2 conjugate leaves, 17.6 x 11.4 cm.; with
envelope. Same paper as 4.12.8.

Same provenance as 4.12.4.

**4.12.11**    A.L.s. to F. Holland Day;
[Madrid], 1 December [1890].

2p. on 2 conjugate leaves, 17.6 x 11.4 cm.; with
envelope. Same paper as 4.12.8.

Same provenance as 4.12.4.

**4.12.12**    A.L.s. to F. Holland Day;
[Madrid, December 1890?].

2p. on 2 conjugate leaves, 17.6 x 11.4 cm.; with
envelope, and printed visiting card of Juan
Enrique de Llanos. Same paper as 4.12.8.

Same provenance as 4.12.4.

**4.12.13**    A.L.s. to F. Holland Day;
[Madrid, December 1890?].

2p. on 2 conjugate leaves, 17.6 x 11.4 cm.; with
envelope. Same paper as 4.12.8.

Same provenance as 4.12.4.

**4.12.14**   A.L.s. to F. Holland Day;
Madrid, 11 January 1891.

7p. on 2 pairs of conjugate leaves, 17.6 x 11.4
cm.; with envelope. Same paper as 4.12.8.

Same provenance as 4.12.4.

**4.12.15**   A.L.s. to F. Holland Day;
Madrid, 25 February 1891.

10p. on 1 leaf and 2 pairs of conjugate leaves,
17.6 x 11.4 cm.; with envelope. Same paper as
4.12.8.

Same provenance as 4.12.4.

**4.12.16**   A.L.s. to F. Holland Day;
Madrid, 9 March 1891.

6p. on 2 leaves and 2 conjugate leaves,
17.6 x 11.4 cm.; with envelope. Same paper as
4.12.8.

Same provenance as 4.12.4.

**4.12.17**   A.L.s. to F. Holland Day;
Madrid, 9 June 1891.

8p. on 2 pairs of conjugate leaves of mourning
paper, 17.4 x 11.4 cm.; with envelope. Laid
paper unwatermarked.

Same provenance as 4.12.4.

**4.12.18**   Typed transcripts of 3 letters to F.
Holland Day; 23 June 1891, 17 May 1893,
13 January 1895. The originals are in the
Dedham Historical Society. The transcripts
were made by Stephen M. Parrish.

## Mathew, George Felton, b. 1795.

**4.13.1**      A.L.s. to Richard Monckton Milnes,
Baron Houghton; Kennington,
12 January [1847]. *KC* 209.

3p. on 2 conjugate leaves, 22.7 x 18.5 cm. Wove
paper unwatermarked.

Same provenance as 1.14. Presented by Arthur A.
Houghton, Jr., 1970.

**4.13.2**   A.L.s. to Richard Monckton Milnes,
Baron Houghton; Kennington, 3 February 1847.
*KC* 212.

6p. on 2 pairs of conjugate leaves, 22.7 x 18.5
cm. Same paper as 4.13.1.

Same provenance as 4.13.1.

**4.13.3**   A.L.s. to Richard Monckton Milnes,
Baron Houghton; Kennington,
11 February 1847. *KC* 215. Includes eight poems
by Mathew. *KC* 216.

6p. on 2 pairs of conjugate leaves, 22.7 x 18.5
cm. Same paper as 4.13.1.

Same provenance as 4.13.1.

**4.13.4**   Mathew, Caroline. A.L.s. to [George
Felton Mathew]; Northam, 9 February 1847.
*KC* 214; forwarded to Milnes with 4.13.3.

4p. on 2 conjugate leaves, 18 x 11.2 cm. Laid
paper watermarked: 1846.

Same provenance as 4.13.1.

**4.13.5**   A.L.s. to [Richard Monckton Milnes,
Baron Houghton]; Kennington, 3 March 1847.
*KC* 219.

3p. on 2 conjugate leaves, 22.7 x 18.5 cm. Same
paper as 4.13.1.

Same provenance as 4.13.1.

**4.13.6**   A.L.s. to Richard Monckton Milnes,
Baron Houghton; Kennington, 5 April 1847.
*KC* 222.

2p. on 2 conjugate leaves, 18.6 x 11.5 cm. Bluish
wove paper unwatermarked.

Same provenance as 4.13.1.

**4.13.7**   Stephens, Henry. MS.L. (transcript) to
George Felton Mathew; [n.p., March 1847?].
*KC* 221; forwarded to Milnes with 4.13.6.

11p. on 6 leaves, 24.7 x 19.4 cm. Blue wove
paper unwatermarked.

Same provenance as 4.13.1.

Stephens's reminiscences of Keats at Guy's Hospital.

**4.13.8**    A.L.s. to [Richard Monckton Milnes, Baron Houghton]; Kennington, 14 August 1848. *KC* 240.

8p. on 2 pairs of conjugate leaves, 22.5 x 17.9 cm. Laid paper watermarked: BACKHOUSE & Cᴼ | 1847.

Same provenance as 4.13.1.

**4.13.9**    A.L.s. to Richard Monckton Milnes, Baron Houghton; [London], 15 August 1848. *KC* 241.

2p. on 2 conjugate leaves, 22.3 x 18 cm. Bluish laid paper watermarked: C HARRIS | 1845.

Same provenance as 4.13.1.

### Reynolds, John Hamilton, 1794–1852.

**4.14.1**    A.L.s. to John Keats; [London, 14 October 1818]. *KC* 19. Rollins 113.

4p. on 2 leaves (formerly conjugate), 18.5 x 11.3 cm. Laid paper, fragment of unidentified watermark.

William Harris Arnold; E. S. Burgess. Presented by Arthur A. Houghton, Jr., 1970.

**4.14.2**    A.L.s. to J. A. Hessey; [London, January 1823]. *KC* 321.

2p. on 2 conjugate leaves, 20.4 x 12.6 cm. Laid paper, fragment of unidentified watermark.

Presented by Donald P. Perry, 1947.

**4.14.3**    A.L.s. to J. A. Hessey; [London, January 1823]. *KC* 322.

3p. on 2 conjugate leaves, 19.9 x 12.5 cm. Laid paper watermarked: LAY.

Same provenance as 4.14.2.

**4.14.4**    A.L.s. to John Taylor; [London, January 1823?]. *KC* 323.

3p. on 2 conjugate leaves, 22.4 x 18.7 cm. Laid paper watermarked with crowned posthorn and script CW.

Same provenance as 4.14.2.

**4.14.5**    A.L.s. to J. A. Hessey; [London, June 1824?]. *KC* 343.

3p. on 2 conjugate leaves, 18.8 x 12.4 cm. Laid paper watermarked: 1820.

Same provenance as 4.14.2.

**4.14.6**    A.L.s. to John Taylor; [London], 15 August 1823. *KC* 335.

2p. on 2 conjugate leaves, 22.9 x 18.7 cm. Laid paper watermarked: GATER | 1819.

Same provenance as 4.14.2.

**4.14.7**    A.L.s. to John Taylor; [London], 31 October 1837. *KC* 347.

3p. on 2 conjugate leaves, 25.5 x 20.5 cm. Laid paper watermarked with triple plume and: [script] J & M | 1835.

Same provenance as 4.14.2.

**4.14.8**    A.L.s. to J. A. Hessey; [London, ca. 1825]. *KC* 135.

1p. on 1 leaf, 23.3 x 19.9 cm. Laid paper watermarked: E S | 1824.

Presented by Arthur A. Houghton, Jr., 1970.

**4.14.9**    A.L.s. to Edward Moxon; [London], 27 November 1846. *KC* 196.

2p. on 2 conjugate leaves, 18.3 x 11.5 cm. Bluish wove paper unwatermarked.

Same provenance as 1.14. Presented by Arthur A. Houghton, Jr., 1970.

**4.14.10**    A.L.s. to Edward Moxon; [London] 15 December 1846. *KC* 199.

4p. on 2 conjugate leaves of mourning paper, 17.7 x 11.1 cm. Wove paper unwatermarked.

Same provenance as 4.14.9.

**4.14.11**    A.L.s. to Richard Monckton Milnes, Baron Houghton; [London], 22 December 1846. *KC* 204.

5p. on 1 leaf and 2 conjugate leaves of

mourning paper, 19.8 x 10.9 cm. Wove paper unwatermarked.

Same provenance as 4.14.9.

**4.14.12**  A.L.s. to Richard Monckton Milnes, Baron Houghton; [London], 30 December [1846]. *KC* 207.

4p. on 2 conjugate leaves, 20 x 12.2 cm. Bluish wove paper unwatermarked.

**4.14.13**  A.L.s. to Richard Monckton Milnes, Baron Houghton; Newport, 2 July 1847. *KC* 231.

7p. on 2 pairs of conjugate leaves, 18.5 x 11.2 cm. Bluish wove paper watermarked: JOYNSON | 1846.

Same provenance as 4.14.9.

**4.14.14**  A.L.s. to Richard Monckton Milnes, Baron Houghton; [London], 17 April 1848. *KC* 233.

4p. on 2 conjugate leaves, 18.2 x 11.2 cm. Bluish wove paper unwatermarked.

Same provenance as 4.14.9.

**4.14.15**  A.L.s. to Richard Monckton Milnes, Baron Houghton; Newport, 22 June [1848]. *KC* 235.

3p. on 2 conjugate leaves of mourning paper, 18.1 x 11.2 cm. Laid paper, fragment of watermark, crowned posthorn.

Same provenance as 4.14.9.

**4.14.16**  A.L.s. to Richard Monckton Milnes, Baron Houghton; Newport, 10 August 1848. *KC* 239.

4p. on 2 conjugate leaves of mourning paper, 22.6 x 18.7 cm. Wove paper unwatermarked.

Same provenance as 4.14.9.

**4.14.17**  Three sonnets: *Robin the outlaw! is there not a mass; The trees of Sherwood Forest are old and good; With coat of Lincoln green and mantle too.*

MS. (transcript, unidentified hand); [n.p., ca. 1847?]. 3p. on 2 conjugate leaves, 24.5 x 20.1 cm. Bluish laid paper watermarked with crowned posthorn and script W.

Same provenance as 4.14.9.

### Severn, Joseph, 1793–1879.

**4.15.1**  A.L.s. to William Haslam; [London, 12 [?] July 1820]. *KC* 56. Rollins 273.

4p. on 2 conjugate leaves, 20 x 16 cm. Laid paper watermarked with lion in crowned oval.

Same provenance as 1.14. Presented by Arthur A. Houghton, Jr., 1970.

**4.15.2**  A.L. to William Haslam; [on shipboard, 19 September 1820]. *KC* 67. Rollins 299.

3p. on 2 conjugate leaves, 18.4 x 15.1 cm. Wove paper unwatermarked.

Same provenance as 4.15.1.

**4.15.3**  A.L. to [William Haslam?]; [on shipboard, 19 September 1820?]. Rollins 300.

1p. on 1 slip of paper, 5.7 x 17.2 cm. Laid paper, portion of Britannia watermark. In Severn's hand, with forged signature of John Keats, evidently a later addition.

Same provenance as 4.15.1.

**4.15.4**  A.L.s. to William Haslam; [on shipboard, 21] September 1820. *KC* 69. Rollins 301.

8p. on 2 pairs of conjugate leaves, 31.5 x 20.1 cm. Laid paper watermarked: [script] R & J | 1818, with countermark of seated Britannia in a crowned oval.

Same provenance as 4.15.1.

**4.15.5**  A.L.s. to William Haslam; Naples, 22 October 1820. *KC* 76. Rollins 304.

3p. on 2 conjugate leaves, 22.5 x 18.2 cm. Wove paper unwatermarked.

Same provenance as 4.15.1.

**4.15.6**    A.L.s. to William Haslam;
Naples, 1–2 November 1820. *KC* 77. Rollins 307.

4p. on 2 conjugate leaves, 31.5 x 20.1 cm. Same
paper as 4.15.4.

Same provenance as 4.15.1.

**4.15.7**    A.L.s. to John Taylor;
Rome, 24 December 1820. *KC* 85.

4p. on 2 conjugate leaves, 25.5 x 20.7 cm. Wove
paper watermarked with parallel lines.
Damaged and repaired, affecting the text in
numerous places.

Bequeathed by Amy Lowell, 1925.

**4.15.8**    A.L.s. to William Haslam;
Rome, 15 January 1821. *KC* 92. Rollins 314.

4p. on 2 conjugate leaves, 25.5 x 20.7 cm. Same
paper as 4.15.7.

Same provenance as 4.15.1.

**4.15.9**    A.L.s. to John Taylor;
Rome, 25 January 1821. *KC* 94. Rollins 315.

4p. on 2 conjugate leaves, 24.6 x 18.9 cm. Wove
paper unwatermarked.

Same provenance as 4.15.7.

**4.15.10**    A.L.s. to William Haslam; Rome, 22
February 1821. *KC* 105. Rollins 317.

4p. on 2 conjugate leaves, 24.6 x 18.9 cm. Same
paper as 4.15.9.

Same provenance as 4.15.1.

**4.15.11**    A.L.s. to John Taylor;
Rome, 6 March 1820. *KC* 107. Rollins 318.

4p. on 2 conjugate leaves, 24.6 x 18.9 cm. Same
paper as 4.15.9.

Bequeathed by Amy Lowell, 1925.

**4.15.12**    A.L.s. to William Haslam;
Rome, 5 May 1821. *KC* 116.

4p. on 2 conjugate leaves, 25.7 x 20.5 cm. Wove
paper watermarked with script C S in wreath.

Same provenance as 4.15.1.

**4.15.13**    A.L.s. to John Taylor;
Rome, 16 May 1821. *KC* 120.

4p. on 2 conjugate leaves, 25.7 x 20.5 cm. Same
paper as 4.15.12.

Same provenance as 4.15.1.

**4.15.14**    A.L.s. to William Haslam;
Rome, 12 July 1821. *KC* 121.

4p. on 2 conjugate leaves, 23.3 x 19.1 cm. Laid
paper watermarked with crowned posthorn.

Bequeathed by Amy Lowell, 1925.

**4.15.15**    MS.L. (transcribed by J. A. Hessey) to
William Haslam; [on shipboard, 21] September
1820. *KC* 69. Rollins 301. Transcript of 4.15.4.

7p. on 2 pairs of conjugate leaves, 32.4 x 20.5
cm. Laid paper watermarked: DUSAUTOY & Cᵒ
| 1818, with countermark of lion in a crowned
oval.

Bequeathed by Amy Lowell, 1925.

**4.15.16**    MS.L. (transcribed by J. A. Hessey) to
William Haslam; Naples, 1 November 1820.
*KC* 77. Rollins 304. Transcript of 4.15.5.

4p. on 2 conjugate leaves, 22.4 x 18.3 cm. Laid
paper watermarked with crowned posthorn
and script J & E G.

Bequeathed by Amy Lowell, 1925.

**4.15.17**    MS.L. (transcribed by J. A. Hessey) to
Charles Armitage Brown;
Rome, 14–17 December 1820. *KC* 84. Rollins 311.

4p. on 2 conjugate leaves, 30.5 x 19.8 cm. Laid
paper watermarked: HOOKE | 1816, with
countermark of lion in crowned oval.

Bequeathed by Amy Lowell, 1925.

**4.15.18**    MS.L. (transcribed by J. A. Hessey) to
[Mrs. Samuel Brawne]; Rome, 11 January 1820.
*KC* 89.

4p. on 2 conjugate leaves, 22.8 x 18.4 cm. Wove
paper unwatermarked.

Bequeathed by Amy Lowell, 1925.

**4.15.19**   MS.L. (transcribed by J. A. Hessey) to William Haslam; Rome, 15 January 1821. *KC* 92. Rollins 314 Transcript of 4.15.8.

4p. on 2 conjugate leaves, 22.8 x 18.4 cm. Same paper as 4.15.18.

Bequeathed by Amy Lowell, 1925.

**4.15.20**   A.L.s. to John Taylor; Rome, 5 January 1822. *KC* 128.

4p. on 2 conjugate leaves, 22.3 x 19 cm. Laid paper watermarked: [script] M | J8J8, with countermark of tall pyramid topped with a circle.

Bequeathed by Amy Lowell, 1925.

**4.15.21**   A.L. (unfinished) to Leigh Hunt; Rome, 21 January 1823.

1p. on 2 conjugate leaves, 24.7 x 18.8 cm. Same paper as 4.15.20.

Presented by Arthur A. Houghton, Jr., 1954.

An account of Shelley's funeral.

**4.15.22**   A.L.s. to William Haslam; Rome, 1 June 1823. *KC* 130.

4p. on 2 conjugate leaves, 23.4 x 18.2 cm. Wove paper watermarked with flowerpot of leaves.

Same provenance as 4.15.1.

**4.15.23**   A.L.s. to John Taylor; [London, March 1841?]. *KC* 167.

4p. on 2 conjugate leaves, 18.3 x 11 cm. Wove paper unwatermarked.

Presented by Lucius Wilmerding, 1946.

**4.15.24**   A.L.s. to Richard Monckton Milnes, Baron Houghton; [London, 27 July 1842]. *KC* 172.

1p. on 2 conjugate leaves, 18.4 x 11.3 cm. Blue laid paper unwatermarked.

Same provenance as 4.15.1.

**4.15.25**   A.L.s. to Richard Monckton Milnes, Baron Houghton; [London], 6 October [1845]. *KC* 181.

6p. on 1 leaf and 2 conjugate leaves, 22.8 x 18.6 cm. Wove paper unwatermarked.

Same provenance as 4.15.1.

**4.15.26**   A.L.s. to Richard Monckton Milnes, Baron Houghton; [London], 13 July [1846?]. *KC* 194.

4p. on 2 conjugate leaves, 18.4 x 11.4 cm. Blue laid paper watermarked: J WHATMAN.

Same provenance as 4.15.1.

**4.15.27**   A.L.s. to Richard Monckton Milnes, Baron Houghton; [London], 5 May [1848]. *KC* 234.

4p. on 2 conjugate leaves, 20.1 x 16 cm. Blue laid paper watermarked with lion in crowned oval.

Same provenance as 4.15.1.

**4.15.28**   A.L.s. to Frederick Locker-Lampson; Rome, 28 April 1862. *KC* 266.

1p. on 1 leaf of mourning paper, 21 x 13.5 cm. Bluish laid paper unwatermarked.

Bequeathed by Amy Lowell, 1925.

**4.15.29**   A.L.s. to Emma Frances Keats Speed; Rome, 1 September 1863. *KC* 267.

4p. on 2 conjugate leaves, 18.5 x 12.3 cm. Laid paper unwatermarked.

William Harris Arnold; E. S. Burgess. Presented by Arthur A. Houghton, Jr., 1970.

**4.15.30**   A.L.s. to Richard Monckton Milnes, Baron Houghton; Rome, 28 September 1864. *KC* 269.

4p. on 2 conjugate leaves, 18.5 x 12.3 cm. Same paper as 4.15.29.

Same provenance as 4.15.1.

**4.15.31**   A.L.s. to Richard Monckton Milnes, Baron Houghton; [Rome, 1867]. *KC* 270.

2p. on 2 conjugate leaves, 18.4 x 11.3 cm. Wove paper, unidentified watermark, embossed consular crest.

Same provenance as 4.15.1.

**4.15.32**   A.L.s. to Richard Monckton Milnes, Baron Houghton; [Rome], 23 March [1868]. *KC* 271.

1p. on 1 leaf, 18.4 x 11.3 cm. Same paper as 4.15.31.

Same provenance as 4.15.1.

**4.15.33**   A.L.s. to Richard Monckton Milnes, Baron Houghton; Rome, 26 October 1869. *KC* 272.

3p. on 2 conjugate leaves, 17.8 x 11.3 cm. Laid paper unwatermarked, with printed consular badge.

Same provenance as 4.15.1.

**4.15.34**   A.L.s. to Richard Monckton Milnes, Baron Houghton; Rome, 8 June 1873. *KC* 274.

3p. on 2 conjugate leaves, 20.6 x 13.2 cm. Laid paper unwatermarked.

Same provenance as 4.15.1.

**4.15.35**   A.L.s. to Eliza W. Field; [Rome] 19 March 1875. *KC* 280.

1p. on 2 conjugate leaves, 16.2 x 13.5 cm. Laid paper unwatermarked.

Same provenance as 4.15.1.

**4.15.36**   A.L.s. to Arthur [Severn]; Rome, 18 February 1877.

1p. on 1 leaf; on verso of original photographic print of Keats's grave, made by Sir Vincent Eyre; 30.8 x 39.5 cm.

Purchased with the Frank B. Bemis Fund, 1953.

**4.15.37**   Holmes, Edward, 1797–1859. A.L.s. to Joseph Severn; London, 23 February 1822.

4p. on 2 conjugate leaves, 22.5 x 18.4 cm. Wove paper watermarked: SMITH & ALLNUTT | 1818.

Presented by Arthur A. Houghton, Jr., 1954.

**4.16.1**   Biographical notes on Keats. *KC* 182.

A.MS. (unsigned; incomplete); [n.p., October 1845?].

10p. on 5 leaves, 19.8 x 16.2 cm. Ruled bluish wove paper unwatermarked.

Same provenance as 1.14. Presented by Arthur A. Houghton, Jr., 1970.

**4.16.2**   On the adversities of Keats's fame.

A.MS.s.; Rome, [25 December] 1861.

21p. on 4 leaves and 6 pairs of conjugate leaves, 25 x 20.5 cm. Blue wove paper unwatermarked. Stitched as a pamphlet.

Presented by Arthur A. Houghton, Jr., 1954.

**4.16.3**   Adonais . . . with notes. . . [the notes only].

A.MS.s.; Rome, 30 August 1873.

18p. on 3 leaves and 7 pairs of conjugate leaves, 31.1 x 21 cm. Wove paper unwatermarked. Stitched.

Intended for a projected illustrated edition of *Adonais* to be published by Macmillan.

Same provenance as 4.16.2.

**4.16.4**   My tedious life.

A.MS.s.; Tossa, September 1863.

48p. on 2 leaves and 21 pairs of conjugate leaves, 31.1 x 21 cm. Same paper as 4.16.3.

Same provenance as 4.16.2.

**4.16.5**   Fragment of a travel journal in Italy in 1822.

A.MS. (unsigned, incomplete); [n.p., n.d.].

2p. on 2 conjugate leaves, 33 x 20.3 cm. Ruled blue wove paper unwatermarked.

Same provenance as 4.16.2.

### Shelley, Percy Bysshe, 1792–1822.

**4.17.1**   A.L.s. to John Keats; Pisa, 27 July 1820. *KC* 57. Rollins 276.

2p. on I leaf, 25.4 x 20.8 cm. Wove paper unwatermarked.

Seymour de Ricci, *A Bibliography of Shelley's Letters* (1927) no. 484: "Given before 1841 by Leigh Hunt to George Henry Lewes who gave it in 1876 to Mrs. Elma Stewart; sale at Sotheby's (2 June 1919, pp. 16-17, n. 106) £ 262 to Quaritch; collection of Miss Amy Lowell, bequeathed in 1925 to Harvard College Library."

### Spurgin, John, 1797–1866.

**4.18.1**   A.L.s. to John Keats; [Cambridge], 5 December [1815].

4p. on 2 conjugate leaves, 21.9 x 18.3 cm. Wove paper watermarked with triple plume and [script] M & J | 1813.

Sold at Sotheby's, 16 December 1958, lot 496. Presented by Arthur A. Houghton, Jr., 1970.

### Hessey, J. A. (James Augustus), 1785–1870.

*see also 4.8.1-.40*

**4.19.1**   A.L.s. to William Haslam; [London], 6–21 October 1820. *KC* 75.

2p. on I leaf, 32.3 x 19.8 cm. Wove paper unwatermarked.

Same provenance as 1.14. Presented by Arthur A. Houghton, Jr., 1970.

**4.19.2**   A.L.s. to William Haslam; [London], 23 November 1820. *KC* 79.

2p. on 2 conjugate leaves, 22.9 x 18.5 cm. Wove paper unwatermarked.

Same provenance as 4.19.1.

**4.19.3**   A.L.s. to William Haslam; [London], 5 December 1820. *KC* 82.

2p. on I leaf, 22.8 x 18.5 cm. Wove paper watermarked: SIMMONS | 1816.

Same provenance as 4.19.1.

**4.19.4**   A.L.s. to William Haslam; [London], 29 January 1821. *KC* 95.

2p. on I leaf, 22.9 x 18.4. Wove paper unwatermarked.

Same provenance as 4.19.1.

**4.19.5**   A.L.s. to William Haslam; [London], 31 January 1821. *KC* 96.

3p. on 2 conjugate leaves, 22.9 x 18.7 cm. Wove paper unwatermarked.

Same provenance as 4.19.1.

**4.19.6**   A.L.s. to Joseph Severn; London, 12 February 1821.

4p. on 2 conjugate leaves, 22.4 x 18.3 cm. Laid paper watermarked with posthorn and script J & E G (same paper as 4.19.9?).

Presented by Arthur A.Houghton, Jr., 1954.

**4.19.7**   A.L.s. to Joseph Severn; London, 27 February 1821.

4p. on 2 conjugate leaves, 22.4 x 18.3 cm. Same paper as 4.19.6.

Same provenance as 4.19.6.

**4.19.8**   A.L.s. to William Haslam; [London], 5 May 1821. *KC* 117.

2p. on I leaf, 22.4 x 18.I cm. Laid paper watermarked: GATER.

Same provenance as 4.19.1.

**4.19.9**   A.L.s. to William Haslam; London, 7 August 1821. *KC* 124.

3p. on 2 conjugate leaves, 22.5 x 18.5 cm. Wove paper watermarked: GATER | 1815.

Same provenance as 4.19.1.

**4.19.10**   A.L.s. to William Haslam;
London, 18 August 1821. *KC* 126.

2p. on 2 conjugate leaves, 22.7 x 18.7 cm. Wove
paper watermarked: BASTED MILL | 1820.

Same provenance as 4.19.1.

*Taylor, John, 1781–1864.*

**4.19.11**   A.L.s. to Richard Woodhouse;
Bakewell, 25 September 1819. *KC* 41.

4p. on 2 conjugate leaves, 22.4 x 18.4 cm. Same
paper as 4.19.6.

Bequeathed by Amy Lowell, 1925.

**4.19.12**   A.L.s. to Michael Drury;
London, 26 January 1820. *KC* 43.

4p. on 2 conjugate leaves, 22.4 x 18.3 cm. Same
paper as 4.19.6.

Bequeathed by Amy Lowell, 1925.

**4.19.13**   A.L.s. to William Haslam;
[London, 13 September 1820]. *KC* 64.

2p. on 2 conjugate leaves, 22.6 x 18 cm. Wove
paper unwatermarked.

Same provenance as 4.19.1.

**4.19.14**   A.L.s. to Joseph Severn;
London, 6 February 1821.

4p. on 2 conjugate leaves, 22.7 x 18.1 cm. Wove
paper watermarked: J WHATMAN | 1819.

Same provenance as 4.19.6.

**4.19.15**   A.L.s. to Michael Drury;
London, 19 February 1821. *KC* 104.

4p. on 2 conjugate leaves, 23.2 x 18.7 cm. Laid
paper watermarked with posthorn and script
J W.

Bequeathed by Amy Lowell, 1925.

**4.19.16**   MS.L. (transcript of 4.19.15 by J. A.
Hessey) to Michael Drury; London,
19 February 1821. *KC* 104.

3p. on 2 conjugate leaves, 20.3 x 19.6 cm. Laid
paper watermarked: HOOKE | 1816, with
countermark of lion in a crowned oval.

Presented by Lucius Wilmerding, 1946.

**4.19.17**   Printed 60-day draft on George Keats,
filled out in MS., drawn by Taylor & Hessey; in
cover addressed to Richard Woodhouse. *KC* 103.

Draft: 1p. on 1 leaf, 8.7 x 23.2 cm. Wove paper
unwatermarked. Cover: 1p. on 1 leaf, 37.1 x 23.1
cm. Laid paper watermarked: J BUDGEN | 1820.

Bequeathed by Amy Lowell, 1925.

**4.19.18**   A.L.s. to Joseph Severn;
London, 3 April 1821.

4p. on 2 conjugate leaves, 23.2 x 18.7 cm. Same
paper as 4.19.15.

Same provenance as 4.19.6.

**4.19.19**   A.L.s. (rough draft) to John Hamilton
Reynolds; [London], 11 June 1824.

3p. on 2 conjugate leaves, 22.8 x 18.5 cm. Wove
paper watermarked: J BUDGEN | 1823.

Purchased with gifts of Friends of the Library, 1947.

**4.19.20**   A.L.s. to Richard Woodhouse;
[London], 20–23 April 1827. *KC* 140.

14p. on 1 leaf and 3 pairs of conjugate leaves,
22.8 x 18.8 cm. Wove paper watermarked:
BASTED MILL | 1824.

Bequeathed by Amy Lowell, 1925.

A report of Richard Abbey's reminiscences of the
Keats family.

**4.19.21**   A.L.s. to Edward Moxon;
[London], 13 February 1845. *KC* 174.

4p. on 2 conjugate leaves, 18.1 x 11.3 cm. Wove
paper watermarked: JOYNSON | 1843.

Same provenance as 4.19.1.

### Taylor & Hessey (firm), London.

**4.19.22**  MS.L. (written by J. A. Hessey) to William Haslam; [London], 12 January 1821. *KC* 90.

2p. on 2 conjugate leaves, 18.7 x 11.4 cm. Wove paper unwatermarked.

Same provenance as 4.19.1.

**4.19.23**  MS.L. (by J. A. Hessey) to William Haslam; [London], 10 February 1821. *KC* 98.

2p. on 2 conjugate leaves, 26.8 x 21 cm. Laid paper watermarked: GATER | 1815.

Same provenance as 4.19.1.

**4.19.24**  MS.L. (by J. A. Hessey) to George Keats; London, 17 February 1821. *KC* 102.

4p. on 2 conjugate leaves, 22.4 x 18.3 cm. Same paper as 4.19.6.

Bequeathed by Amy Lowell, 1925.

**4.19.25**  MS.L. (by J. A. Hessey; duplicate of 4.19.17 and 4.19.24) to George Keats; London, 17 February 1821. *KC* 102, 103.

4p. on 2 conjugate leaves, 22.9 x 18.6 cm. Laid paper watermarked: PHIPPS & SONS | 1818.

Same provenance as 4.19.16.

**4.19.26**  MS.L. (by J. A. Hessey) to William Haslam; [London], 17 February 1821. *KC* 101.

2p. on 2 conjugate leaves, 22.7 x 18.3 cm. Wove paper unwatermarked.

Same provenance as 4.19.1.

**4.19.27**  MS.L. (by J. A. Hessey) to William Haslam; [London], 9 March 1821. *KC* 109.

2p. on 2 conjugate leaves, 23 x 18.5 cm. Laid paper watermarked with posthorn and unidentified script monogram.

Same provenance as 4.19.1.

### Woodhouse, Richard, 1788–1834.

**4.20.1**  A.L.s. (rough draft) to John Keats; [London], 21 October 1818. *KC* 21. Rollins 115.

4p. on 2 conjugate leaves, 25.3 x 20.2 cm. Laid paper watermarked with posthorn and unidentified script monogram. Silked.

Bequeathed by Amy Lowell, 1925.

**4.20.2**  A.L.s. to John Keats; [London], 10 December 1818. *KC* 32. Rollins 126.

3p. on 2 conjugate leaves, 22.5 x 18.3 cm. Laid paper watermarked: C WILMOTT | 1814.

Bequeathed by Amy Lowell, 1925.

**4.20.3**  Porter, Jane, 1776-1850. MS.L. (transcribed by Richard Woodhouse) to William Henry Neville; Ditton Cottage, 4 December 1818. *KC* 29.

2p. on 2 conjugate leaves, 22.6 x 18.4 cm. Laid paper watermarked: GATER | 1815. Sent to Keats with 4.20.2.

Bequeathed by Amy Lowell, 1925.

**4.20.4**  A.L.s. to John Keats; [London], 16 September 1820. *KC* 66. Rollins 297.

2p. on 2 conjugate leaves, 23.5 x 19.2 cm. Wove paper unwatermarked.

Bequeathed by Amy Lowell, 1925.

**4.20.5**  Critique of *When I have fears that I may cease to be. KC* 59.

A.MS. (draft, unsigned); [n.p., n.d.].

2p. on 1 leaf, 22.7 x 18.5 cm. Laid paper with fragment of posthorn watermark.

Bequeathed by Amy Lowell, 1925.

## Woodhouse, Richard, 1788–1834, transcriber.

*Additional Woodhouse transcripts are found in III.*

**4.20.6**   Keats, John. MS.L. (transcribed by Woodhouse) to John Taylor; Winchester, [23 August 1819]. Rollins 183.

2p. on 1 leaf, 23.5 x 19.1 cm. Wove paper unwatermarked.

Bequeathed by Amy Lowell, 1925.

**4.20.7**   Keats, John. MS.L. (transcribed by Woodhouse) to John Taylor; Winchester, 1 September [i.e. 31 August] 1819. Rollins 188. With: MS.L. (transcribed by same) to J. A. Hessey; Winchester, 5 September 1819. Rollins 189.

1p. on 1 leaf, 23.5 x 19.1 cm. Wove paper unwatermarked.

Bequeathed by Amy Lowell, 1925.

**4.20.8**   *Fanatics have their dreams, wherewith they weave* ["The Fall of Hyperion"].

MS. (transcribed by clerk, with notes by Richard Woodhouse); [n.p., n.d.].

16p. on 8 leaves, 32.6 x 20.3 cm. Laid paper watermarked: C WILMOT | 1833, with countermark of lion in crowned oval.

Same provenance as 1.14. Presented by Arthur A. Houghton, Jr., 1970.

**4.20.9**   Transcripts of poems, as follows:
*As from the darkening gloom a silver dove*
*Oh! how I love, on a fair summer's eve*
*After dark vapours have oppressed our plains*
*Fresh morning gusts have blown away all fear*
*This pleasant tale is like a little copse*
*Blue! 'tis the life of heaven—the domain*
*It keeps eternal whisperings around*
*Time's sea hath been five years at its slow ebb*
*Mother of Hermes! and still youthful Maia*
*Spenser, a jealous honourer of thine*

*Four seasons fill the measure of the year*
*Oh Chatterton, how very sad thy fate*
*Byron, how sweetly sad thy melody*
*O that a week could be a year, and we*
*Stay, ruby breasted warbler, stay*
*O come, my dear Emma, the rose is full blown*
*O peace! and dost thou with thy presence bless*
*In thy western halls of gold*
*Fill for me a brimming bowl*
*Come hither all sweet maidens, soberly*
*The day is gone, and all its sweets are gone*

MS. (transcribed by clerk, with notes and last two poems transcribed by Richard Woodhouse); [n.p., n.d.].

15p. on 8 leaves, 32.6 x 20.3 cm. Originally the latter part of 4.20.8, and on the same paper; last verso docketed by Woodhouse, "Hyperion b(remodelled) with minor poems."

Same provenance as 4.20.8.

**4.20.10**   Transcripts of poems, as follows:
*God of the golden bow*
*It keeps eternal whisperings around*
*Time's sea hath been five years at its slow ebb*
*When I have fears that I may cease to be*
*After dark vapours have oppressed our plains*
*My spirit is too weak! Mortality*
*Haydon! forgive me that I cannot speak*
*Blue! 'tis the hue [life] of Heaven—the domain*

MS. (transcribed by Richard Woodhouse); [n.p., n.d.].

6p. on 3 leaves, 20.7 x 13.1 cm. Wove paper watermarked: J WHATMAN | 1830.

Presented by Arthur A. Houghton, Jr., 1954.

**4.20.11**   Woodhouse, Richard. Journal, recording literary opinions and table-talk; 28 September–29 December 1821.

55p. on 32 leaves, 24.3 x 19.7 cm.; at least 4 leaves excised at beginning; numerous blank leaves after text. Laid paper watermarked: TAVERHAM | 1807, countermarked with fleur-de-lys with T in top petal. Signed and dated by Woodhouse on first flyleaf, 1 January 1812; again on verso, 19 November 1821, with note: "In the Event of my death, whenever it shall happen, I desire that this book may be given to Mr. Taylor of Fleet Street." Green vellum binding.

Most of the journal records the table-talk of Thomas De Quincey. Includes De Quincey's opinion that the review in *Blackwood's* of *Endymion* was written by John Wilson (f.4ᵛ).

Purchased from Miss M. Craig, as the gift of Ellery Sedgwick, 1954.

★ ★ ★

MS Keats 5, Ancillary Collections, was a short-lived classification, now discontinued. It is not included in this catalogue.

# V. FORGERIES

## 6.1

### *Pleasures lie thickest where no pleasures seem*

MS. signed J. Keats. 1p. on 2 conjugate leaves, 22.6 x 18.8 cm. Laid paper watermarked: J WHATMAN | 1849.

Annotated by Richard Monckton Milnes, "I take this to be one of George Byron's forgeries." But G. Byron never went so far astray in the paper he employed. Theodore G. Ehrsam, *Major Byron* (1952), p.102, identifies the author of the text as [Samuel] Laman Blanchard (1804-1845), and says that he believes G. Byron simply forged the supposed Keats signature to an existing manuscript; but the signature appears to be in the same hand as the text, and it seems more probable that the forger (whoever he was) manufactured the whole thing. Another specimen similarly signed is in the British Museum (Add. MS. 44919); a tracing of it accompanies the present manuscript.

Same provenance as 1.14. Presented by Arthur A. Houghton, Jr., 1970.

## 6.2

### *What sylph-like form before my eyes*

MS. signed J. Keats. 7p. on 2 leaves and 2 conjugate leaves, 18.3 x 15.1 cm. Laid paper watermarked on the conjugate pair with seated Britannia on a crescent; on the disjunct pair: DARK | 1801.

A forgery by G. Byron; source of text unknown, but not by Keats.

Sold at the John Wilks sale, which included numer-ous forgeries (Sotheby, 12 May 1851, lot 1166) to Richard Monckton Milnes; same provenance as 6.1.

Printed by Monckton Milnes as "A fragment of Keats, of doubtful authenticity," in *Life and Letters. . . New edition* (1867) pp. 360-363.

## 6.3

### L.s. John Keats, to W. [*sic*] Haydon; Leatherhead, 20 November 1817.

4p. on 2 conjugate leaves, 19.7 x 16 cm. Laid paper watermarked: E SMITH | 1817. Red wax seal of clasped hands with motto: TO MEET IS SWEET.

A forgery by G. Byron; sources of text unknown, but not based on any genuine text of Keats.

Sold in the Wilks sale (Sotheby, 12 May 1851, lot 1163) to Richard Monckton Milnes; same provenance as 6.1.

Printed as genuine by Monckton Milnes in *Life and Letters. . . New edition* (1867) pp. 49-51.

## 6.4

### L.s. J. Keats, to W. Spencer; Oxford, September 1818.

4p. on 2 conjugate leaves, 19.7 x 16.1 cm. Laid paper watermarked: J BUDGEN | 1816. Red wax seal.

A forgery by G. Byron; source of text unknown, but not based on any genuine text of Keats.

Sold in the Wilks sale (Sotheby, 12 May 1851, lot 1162) to Richard Monckton Milnes; same provenance as 6.1.

Printed as genuine by Monckton Milnes in *Life and Letters. . . New edition* (1867) pp. 27-28.

**6.5**
**L.s. P. B. Shelley, to John Keats;**
**Pisa, 20 July 1820.**

6p. on 1 leaf and 2 conjugate leaves, 26.8 x 20.7
cm. Wove paper unwatermarked.

Same provenance as 6.1.

A forgery; source of text unknown. Page 1
annotated in pencil, "I suspect this to be one of
G. Byron's forgeries—F[rancis] T[urner]
P[algrave]." Palgrave was among the first to
detect G. Byron's forgeries in the 1852 Shelley
*Letters*.

# NAME INDEX

*References are given to MS Keats numbers.*

# CONCORDANCE OF MS KEATS 2
# NUMBERS AND FIRST LINES

2.1     *Hast thou from the caves of Golconda, a gem*

2.2     *Small, busy flames play through the fresh laid coals* and *Many the wonders I this day have seen*

2.3     *Many the wonders I this day have seen*

2.4     *Much have I travell'd in the realms of gold*

2.5     *Small, busy flames play through the fresh laid coals* and *I stood tip-toe upon a little hill*

2.6     *Small, busy flames play through the fresh laid coals*

2.7     *Great spirits now on earth are sojourning*

2.8.1 | *I stood tip-toe upon a little hill*
2.8.2 |
2.8.3 |
2.8.4 |

2.9     *I stood tip-toe upon a little hill*

2.10    *The church bells toll a melancholy round*

2.11    *Happy is England! I could be content*

2.12    *Come hither all sweet maidens, soberly*

2.13    *God of the golden bow*

2.14    *Which of the fairest three*

2.15.1  *Chief of organic numbers!*
2.15.2

2.16    *Souls of poets dead and gone*

2.17.1 | *Fair Isabel, poor simple Isabel!*
2.17.2 |
2.17.3 |
2.17.4 |
2.17.5 |

2.18    *O that a week could be an age, and we*

2.19    *There is a joy in footing slow across a silent plain*

2.20    *Hush, hush! tread softly! hush, hush, my dear*

2.21    *St. Agnes' Eve—Ah, bitter chill it was*

2.22    *Shed no tear—O shed no tear!*

2.23    *Happy, happy glowing fire*

2.24.1 | *So, I am safe emerged from these broils*
2.24.2 |
2.24.3 |
2.24.4 |
2.24.5 |
2.24.6 |
2.24.7 |

2.25    *Upon a time, before the faery broods*

2.26    *Upon a time, before the faery broods*

2.27    *Season of mists and mellow fruitfulness*

2.28    *If shame can on a soldier's vein-swoll'n front*

2.29.1  *In midmost Ind, beside Hydaspes cool*

2.29.2  *In midmost Ind, beside Hydaspes cool* and *This living hand, now warm and capable*

2.30    *Physician Nature! let my spirit blood!*

2.31    *O grant that like to Peter I*

# CONCORDANCE OF TITLES
# AND FIRST LINES

Acrostic
*Give me your patience, sister, while I frame*

Addressed to Haydon
*Highmindedness, a jealousy for good*

Addressed to the Same
*Great spirits now on earth are sojourning*

Answer to a Sonnet. . .
*Blue!—'Tis the life of heaven—the domain*

Apollo to the Graces
*Which of the fairest three*

Calidore
*Young Calidore is paddling o'er the lake*

The Cap and Bells
*In midmost Ind, beside Hydaspes cool*

Character of C.B. [Charles Brown]
*He was to weet a melancholy carle*

Endymion
*A thing of beauty is a joy forever*

The Eve of St. Agnes
*St. Agnes' Eve—Ah, bitter chill it was*

The Eve of St. Mark
*Upon a Sabbath day it fell*

Extracts from an Opera
*O were I one of the Olympian twelve*

Faery Song
*Ah! woe is me! poor Silver-wing!*

Fairy's Song
*Shed no tear—O shed no tear!*

The Fall of Hyperion
*Fanatics have their dreams, wherewith they weave*

Fancy
*Ever let the Fancy roam*

Fragment
*Where's the Poet? Show him! show him!*

Fragment of Castle-builder
*In short, convince you that however wise*

Hyperion: A Fragment
*Deep in the shady sadness of a vale*

Imitation of Spenser
*Now Morning from her orient chamber came*

Isabella; or, The Pot of Basil
*Fair Isabel, poor simple Isabel!*

The Jealousies
*In midmost Ind, beside Hydaspes cool*

King Stephen
*If shame can on a soldier's vein-swoll'n front*

La Belle Dame sans Merci: A Ballad
*O what can ail thee, knight at arms*

Lamia
*Upon a time, before the faery broods*

Lines on Seeing a Lock of Milton's Hair
*Chief of organic numbers!*

Lines on the Mermaid Tavern
*Souls of poets dead and gone*

Lines Rhymed in a Letter from Oxford
*The Gothic looks solemn*

Lines  Written in the Highlands After a Visit to Burns's Country
*There is a joy in footing slow across a silent plain*

Modern Love
*And what is Love?—It is a doll dress'd up*

Nebuchadnezzar's Dream
*Before he went to live with owls and bats*

Ode
*Bards of passion and of mirth*

Ode on a Grecian Urn
*Thou still unravish'd bride of quietness*

Ode on Indolence
*One morn before me were three figures seen*

Ode on Melancholy
*No, no, go not to Lethe, neither twist*

Ode on Melancholy; cancelled first stanza
*Though you should build a bark of dead men's bones*

Ode to a Nightingale
*My heart aches, and a drowsy numbness pains*

Ode to Apollo
This title is given to two poems, beginning: *God of the golden bow* and *In thy western halls of gold*

Ode to May
*Mother of Hermes! and still youthful Maia!*

Ode to Psyche
*O Goddess! hear these tuneless numbers, wrung*

On a Dream
*As Hermes once took to his feathers light*

On a Leander Which Miss Reynolds, My Kind Friend, Gave Me
*Come hither all sweet maidens, soberly*

On Fame
This title is given to two poems, beginning: *Fame, like a wayward girl, will still be coy* and *How fever'd is the man who cannot look*

On First Looking into Chapman's Homer
*Much have I travell'd in the realms of gold*

On Leaving Some Friends at an Early Hour
*Give me a golden pen, and let me lean*

On Peace
*Oh Peace! and dost thou with thy presence bless*

On Receiving a Curious Shell, and a Copy of Verses, from the Same Ladies
*Hast thou from the caves of Golconda, a gem*

On Receiving a Laurel Crown from Leigh Hunt
*Minutes are flying swiftly; and as yet*

On Seeing the Elgin Marbles
*My spirit is too weak—mortality*

On Sitting Down to Read *King Lear* Once Again
*O golden-tongued Romance, with serene lute!*

On the Grasshopper and Cricket
*The poetry of earth is never dead*

On the Sea
*It keeps eternal whisperings around*

On 'The Story of Rimini'
*Who loves to peer up at the morning sun*

On Visiting Staffa
*Not Aladdin magian*

On Visiting the Tomb of Burns
*The town, the churchyard, and the setting sun*

Otho the Great
*So, I am safe emerged from these broils*

Robin Hood
*No! those days are gone away*

Sleep and Poetry
*What is more gentle than a wind in sum-*
*mer?*

Song
This title is given to five poems,
beginning: *Hence burgundy, claret, and*
*port*
*Hush, hush, tread softly, hush, hush, my*
*dear*
*I had a dove, and the sweet dove died*
*O blush not so! O blush not so!*
*Spirit here that reignest!*

Song of Four Fairies
*Happy, happy glowing fire*

Sonnet to Sleep
*O soft embalmer of the still midnight*

Specimen of an Induction to a Poem
*Lo! I must tell a tale of chivalry*

Stanzas
This title is given to two poems, begin-
ning: *In drear nighted December* and
*You say you love; but with a voice*

To * * * *
*Hadst thou liv'd in days of old*

To * * * * *
*Had I a man's fair form, then might my sighs*

To ———
*Time's sea hath been five years at its slow*
*ebb*

To a Friend Who Sent Me Some Roses
*As late I rambled in the happy fields*

To a Young Lady Who Sent Me a Laurel Crown
*Fresh morning gusts have blown away all*
*fear*

To Ailsa Rock
*Hearken, thou craggy ocean pyramid*

To Autumn
*Season of mists and mellow fruitfulness*

To Charles Cowden Clarke
*Oft have you seen a swan superbly frowning*

To Chatterton
*Oh Chatterton! how very sad thy fate*

To Emma
*O come, dearest Emma! the rose is full blown*

To Fanny
*Physician Nature! let my spirit blood!*

To George Felton Mathew
*Sweet are the pleasures that to verse belong*

To G.A.W. [Georgiana Augusta Wylie]
*Nymph of the downward smile, and sidelong*
*glance*

To Haydon
*Great spirits now on earth are sojourning*

To Haydon with a Sonnet Written on Seeing
the Elgin Marbles
*Forgive me, Haydon, that I cannot speak*

To Homer
*Standing aloof in giant ignorance*

To Hope
*When by my solitary hearth I sit*

To J. H. Reynolds, Esq.
*Dear Reynolds, as last night I lay in bed*

To J. R. [James Rice]
*O that a week could be an age, and we*

To Kosciusko
*Good Kosciusko, thy great name alone*

To Leigh Hunt, Esq.
*Glory and loveliness have passed away*

To Lord Byron
*Byron, how sweetly sad thy melody*

JOHN KEATS

1795–1995

was

designed by Duncan Todd.

One thousand two hundred copies

were  printed by Mercantile Printing Company

on 70 lb. Monodnock Dulcet Text

and 100 lb. Monadnock

Dulcet Cover.